Layman's Guide

to

Irish Law

Criminal Law

A plain English guide to criminal law in Ireland

By Teresa Clyne BA, MSc

"To all who dream in part, in the hope that they may attain someone else's experience in the delights and dangers of adventure. Also, to my amazing kids and grandkids for without whose endless empathy, sympathy and encouragement this book would have been finished in half the time". ~

Teresa Clyne

An Introduction to Criminal Law in Ireland

Introduction

What is Criminal Law all about? Before you start this booklet, think about criminal law for a moment, can you write a 4 – 6 sentence paragraph on your interpretation of what criminal law is all about? Take a look at the illustration on your right..!! What does this tell you? Generally criminal law can be described as a set of rules, developed over a long period of time that regulates how individuals interact within society. These standards and laws are enforceable through sanctions which have been enacted by the Government to ensure stability of behaviours within society. There are several presumptions in criminal law and the major ones are

The Presumption of Innocence:

This is the principle that a person charged with a crime is presumed to be innocent. The DPP (state) is responsible to prove the defendant guilty.

The Burden of Proof:

This principle states that the defendant must be released unless the state proves guilt *beyond a reasonable doubt that they are guilty.*

Habeas Corpus:

This principle states a suspect has the right not to be detained or imprisoned unlawfully and if the state can't show cause, the person must be released. So what have we got Criminal Law then? Criminal law is needed inside society, to ensure that society lives in harmony, citizens give certain freedoms in return for protection, the greater good, otherwise known as Utilitarianism, the greater good, and the reasons for criminal laws are:

● Law keeps order in society
● Helps to deter crime my ordering penalties to those who breach society's laws
● It is not about compensation, it is about deterrence

- The Public wants criminal laws so that they feel safer in their homes in societies when wrongdoers are punished and off the "streets".
- There is mixed public opinion on they want to punish or rehabilitate offenders.

What does the law set out to do?

1. Maintains order in society
2. Encourages social change
3. Protects individual rights
4. Enforces moral beliefs
5. Redress' wrongs
6. Identifies wrongdoers
7. Dictates punishment and retribution

Can you think of any other purposes of law?

Finally, there are two separate areas of criminal law;

1. Substantive law: this is the area of law which is regulated by the laws, the statutes, rules, regulations etc.
2. Procedural law: this regulates how the laws are applied by the state, i.e. how the rules are enforced.

This booklet has been compiled to give you a baseline interpretation of all major aspects of Criminal law in Ireland, "the bones" you could call it, it is not intended to be a complete breakdown of Criminal law. This publication is for guidance purposes only. It is not defined as an academic book. It does not constitute legal or professional advice.

An Introduction to Criminal Law in Ireland

Disclaimer: *No liability is accepted by Teresa Clyne for any action taken or not taken in reliance on the information set out in this publication. Any and all information is subject to change and professional or legal advice should be obtained before taking or refraining from any action as a result of the contents of this publication. This booklet is intended to help lay (non-legal) persons who want to understand the Criminal law without taking courses, it is also for students who are in year one of their ACCA, ATI, LLB, King's Inns or FE1 entry exams and who are finding it difficult to understand and comprehend the basic entry principles of the Criminal law, this booklet also helps those who wish to know more about the Criminal law for personal, educational or business reasons. All rights reserved*

An Introduction to Criminal Law in Ireland

Contents

Introduction 2

Criminal Law 4

Chapter one 5

The Main Elements of a Crime 6

Actus Reus 6

Mens Rea 8

Intention 8

What is Criminal Law? 10

Article 38 of the constitution of Ireland provides: 10

Article 40 of the constitution of Ireland 10

Minor and non-minor offences 14

Serious and non-serious offences 15

Accomplice to Crime 15

Principal in Crime 15

Accessory after the Fact 16

Differences between Crimes and Torts 17

Inchoate Offences 18

Attempt 18

Public order offences in Ireland 19

Intoxication (being drunk) in a public place 20

Disorderly conduct in a public place 20

Threatening, abusive or insulting behaviour in a public place 22

Begging in an intimidating or threatening manner 22

Distribution or display in a public place of material which is threatening, abusive, insulting or obscene 23

Failure to comply with the direction of a member of An Garda Siochana .. 23

Wilful obstruction 23

Entering a building, etc., with intent to commit an offence 24

Trespass on land /a building, etc. 24

Riot 25

Violent disorder 25

Affray 26

Blackmail, extortion and demanding money with menaces 26

Assault with intent to cause bodily harm or commit an indictable offence .. 27

Assault or obstruction of a peace officer 28

Attacks on emergency service personnel 28

Chapter 2 30

An Introduction to Criminal Law in Ireland

The Criminal Court System, Arrest and Detention 30
The functions of the Gardaí 32
The Function of the Courts 32
An Introduction to the Irish Court System 33
The District Court in Ireland 34
District Criminal Court 35
The Small Claims Court 37
The Circuit Court in Ireland 38
The High Court in Ireland 40
The Special Criminal Court in Ireland 42
The Court of Appeal in Ireland 43
The Supreme Court in Ireland 46
The Children's Court 47
Personnel involved in the court room 48
Civil Liability & Courts Act 2004 49
The Irish Prison Service 50
Probation Service and the Irish Criminal Justice System 53
Function of the Director of Public Prosecutions 55
Indictable offences: 57
Summary offences: 57
The Prosecution of Crime 59
District Court Summons Procedure 59
The Validity of the Summons 59
Time Limits for the Issuing of A Summons 59
Indictable Offences Time Limits 60
Charge Sheet Procedure 60
Right to Silence and against Self-incrimination 61
Bail 61
Arrest Defined 62
Arrests 62
Arrest without a warrant 62
Entry and search of a premises to carry out an arrest 63
Manner of Arrest 63
Search of the Arrested Person 64
Procedure after Arrest 64
Immunity from Arrest 65
An arrestable offence under the Criminal Law Act 1997 65
Section 30 of the Offences Against The State Act 1939 65

Periods of Detention:...65
Section 30 of the Offences Against the State Act 1939 66
Section 4 of the Criminal Justice Act 1984...66
Section 2 - Drug Trafficking Act 1996..70
Drug offences 70
Customs National Drug Team 71
Possession of any other controlled drugs...72
Growing cannabis plants or opium poppies 72
Regulations regarding opium..72
Possession of controlled drugs for sale or supply 73
Use of premises, vehicles or vessels for certain activities......................73
Forged or fraudulently altered prescriptions 74
Attempting or helping others to commit an offence 74
Court-ordered drug treatment 74
Chapter 3..76
Homicide 76
The Definition of Homicide 76
What is Murder? 78
What is Manslaughter?...78
Voluntary Manslaughter:..78
Section 4 of the Criminal Justice Act, 1964, which provides: 79
A life sentence is mandatory for murder..80
Capital Punishment..81
Death Penalty Facts 81
Manslaughter and Provocation 82
Fatal Assault Manslaughter 83
Criminal Negligence 84
Duty to Act 84
Act or Omission 84
Euthanasia..87
Non-voluntary Euthanasia 87
Assisted Suicide..87
Physician Assisted Suicide..87
Abortion 87
Infanticide 88
Chapter 4..89
Theft, Burglary, Aggravated Burglary and Robbery 90
Section 4 of the Criminal Justice Act 2001...90
Actus Reus and Mens Rea of theft..92

Theft, robbery and burglary.. 93
Aggravated burglary s. 13 the Criminal Justice Act 2001 96
Penalty s. 13(3) the Criminal Justice Act 2001... 98
Section 14 Criminal Justice Act 2001 98
Chapter 5... 99
Defences to a Crime.. 100
The purposes of a defence to a crime 100
The defence of Infancy 100
The defence of Intoxication 101
Intoxication by Drugs 102
The Burden of Proof... 102
Defence of Mistake 103
Defence of Insanity 103
Fit or unfit to be tried 104
Not guilty by reason of insanity 104
Diminished responsibility in murder cases 105
The M'Naghten Rules... 106
Daniel M'Naghten 106
Defence of Automatism... 107
Insane automatism 108
Constrained Choice 109
Defence of Necessity 109
Defence of Coercion 111
About the Author:... 125

An Introduction to Criminal Law in Ireland

Criminal Law

In Ireland, there are approx. 670 crimes committed every day, and alarmingly those do not include motoring offences (central statistics office), with theft accounting for over 30% of those crimes. Criminal law is mainly aimed at controlling behaviours within society.

The purpose of this introductory booklet is to provide readers with a outline understanding of the principles of criminal law in Ireland and to enable them to appreciate the role of criminal law in their personal and vocational lives. It is also intended to prepare readers for their personal lives or further study in related areas.

Readers who complete this booklet will:

- develop a general understanding of the Irish Criminal System
- develop an appreciation of the elements required for a crime to be committed
- evaluate the impact of relevant legislation governing the various aspects of criminal law to be investigated
- acquire skills in evaluation and analysis
- be familiar with the language and procedures related to the various aspects of criminal law studied.

Chapter one

An Introduction to Criminal Law in Ireland

The Main Elements of a Crime

Most crimes comprise two elements, an Actus Reus (*"guilty act"*) and a Mens Rea (*"guilty mind"*).

Actus non facitreum nisi mens sit rea. Correctly translated, this means ***"An act does not make a man guilty of a crime, unless his mind be also guilty."***

ASSAULT & BATTERY

There MUST be a guilty intent and a guilty act present at the same time

ACTUS REUS

Intent — MENS REA

Act

If you merely push someone with no intent to harm them, then this is not Assault or Battery, if you hurt someone with no intent this may be defined as a negligent act

Therefore, it is not the actus which is "reus" but the man and his mind separately. All crimes require proof of an Actus Reus.

Also, there is a presumption that each part of the Actus Reus requires proof of a corresponding Mens Rea. Offences to which the presumption of Mens Rea does not apply are called crimes of strict liability.

(**Example**: *Strict liability means that no intention on behalf of the wrongdoer is needed, such as motoring offences, drink-driving, speeding etc, therefore prosecution need not prove you intended to speed to convict you of speeding contrary to the Road Traffic Act.*)

Actus Reus

> *Actus Reus of an offence consists of:*
> *1) a voluntary*
> *2) act*
> *3) that causes*
> *4) social harm.*

"The Guilty Act". An Actus Reus always includes conduct (*behaviour*) on the part of the *Defendant* (suspect). It may also include a particular circumstance or particular set of circumstances (*things that happened* or things the suspect did), and/or a particular result caused by the suspect's conduct. *Supposing "A" shoots and kills an on-duty member of the Garda Siochana and is consequently charged with murder under **s 3 of the Criminal Justice Act 1990**.* In order to secure a conviction the prosecution would have to prove, inter alia (*amongst other things*), the following Actus Reus:

1. The act of shooting (*conduct*),
2. That the victim was an on-duty member of An Garda Siochana(*circumstance*), and
3. The death of the victim (*result*).

There is no legal punishment for mere thoughts and no person can be prosecuted for thinking bad thoughts.

Mens Rea

"The Guilty Mind". As a general rule, each part of an Actus Reus (*conduct, circumstance and result*) requires proof of a corresponding Mens Rea (*guilty mind*) on the part of the offender. If at least one part of an Actus Reus does not require proof of a corresponding Mens Rea on the part of the suspect, the offence is one of strict liability. The prosecution (DPP) must prove that the suspect had intended the conduct.

Let us return to our example of "A" shooting and killing an on-duty member of An Garda Siochana and being charged with murder contrary to **s 3 of the Criminal Justice Act 1990.** To secure "A's conviction, the Prosecution would have to prove, inter alia, (*amongst other things*) the following Actus Reus:

- That A shot the victim (*conduct*),
- That the victim was an on-duty member of An Garda Siochana (*circumstance*), and
- That the death of the victim (*result*) was caused by A's conducted.

Each part of this *Actus Reus* requires proof of a corresponding *Mens Rea*. So, it would have to be proved that A's conduct was *deliberate* or *voluntary*. If **A** shot the victim whilst sleepwalking, he would be entitled to an acquittal on the ground of automatism. In addition, it would have to be proved that **A** either *knew of the circumstance or was reckless as to its existence*, *i.e. that he knew the victim was on on-duty Garda, or was reckless as to whether or not the victim was an on-duty member of An Garda Siochana.* Finally, it would have to be proved that **A** *intended to kill or to cause serious injury to some person, whether the person actually killed or not.*

Intention

In People **(DPP) v Douglas and Hayes (1985)** the Court of Criminal Appeal considered the meaning of "intention" in the context of **s 14 of the Offences Against the Person Act 1861**, which provides, *"whosoever shall shoot at any person with intent to commit murder, shall, whether any bodily injury be effected or not, be guilty of a felony"*

The applicants had been convicted in the Special Criminal Court of; inter alia, an offence contrary to *s. 14 of the 1861 Act*. They succeeded in arguing that the intent required by s. 14 had not been proved. **McWilliam J** delivered the judgment of the court, saying, *"Unless the suspect has actually expressed intent,* *his intent can only be ascertained from a consideration of his actions and the surrounding circumstances".*

*(**Example**: In order for a person to be guilty of theft they must take an item of property belonging to another person (guilty act), they must also intend (guilty mind) that they deprive that person of it and keep it for themselves).*

What then is the difference between criminal law and civil law?.

Criminal law *– This is the punishment of wrongdoers by the state (maintaining social order)*

Civil law *– This deals with the compensation of losses; system of rights and remedies for regulating interaction between members of society.*

An Introduction to Criminal Law in Ireland

What is Criminal Law?

Criminal law governs crimes. Crimes are generally referred to as offences against the state. It is an offence against the community at large, not an individual. The standard of proof for crimes is "*beyond a reasonable doubt.*" A crime is defined in law in Ireland as an act which may be punished by the State. The way in which a criminal offence is investigated and prosecuted depends on the type of crime involved. For these purposes criminal offences may be described in different ways such as:

- Summary offences
- Indictable offences
- Minor offences
- Serious offences
- Arrestable offences

There are two ways criminal offences can be tried in Irish law:

- In the lower (minor) court (District Court) before a judge **without** a jury (summary).

- In the higher (major) courts (Circuit Criminal Court, Central Criminal Court) before a judge and jury (indictable).

Article 38 of the constitution of Ireland provides:

1. No person shall be tried on any criminal charge save in due course of law
2. Minor offences may be tried by courts of summary jurisdiction
3. Save in the case of trial of offences under section 2 no person shall be tried on any criminal charge without a jury

This constitutional article determines that unless a matter is summary (not very serious, i.e. TV licence, parking, speeding, car tax etc.) then it must be dealt with before a judge and jury.

Article 40 of the constitution of Ireland

Section 3, Subsection 1(1) The State guarantees in its laws to respect, and, as far as practicable, by its laws to defend and vindicate the personal rights of the citizen.

Subsection (1) the State only guarantees to "respect, and, as far as practicable, by its laws defend and vindicate the personal rights of the citizen." In today's society it can be asked, is **as far as practicable** enough to ensure the State protects its citizens.

Section3. Subsection (2) The State shall, in particular, by its laws protect as best it may from unjust attack and, in the case of injustice done; vindicate the life, person, good name, and property rights of every citizen.

Subsection (2) refers only to one set of rights, namely the property rights of every citizen. What it undertakes to protect (against unjust attack) and vindicate (in the case of injustice done) are simply every citizen's life, person and good name, not the right to life, the right to good name.

An Introduction to Criminal Law in Ireland

Classification of Offences

Treason, Felony and Misdemeanour

In Ireland there were THREE (3) classes of criminal offence, treason, felony and misdemeanour. Treason was defined and classified as a felony; however it also was a class of its own.

Under Article 39 of the Irish Constitution:- *"Treason shall consist only in levying war against the State, or assisting any State or person or inciting or conspiring with any person to levy war against the State, or attempting by force of arms or other violent means to overthrow the organs of government established by this Constitution, or taking part or being concerned in or inciting or conspiring with any person to make or to take part or be concerned in any such attempt."*

So what then was a felony?, a felony was a crime which traditionally saw the suspect arrested without a warrant, it was the highest type of crime, **section 3 of the Criminal Law Act 1997** abolished felony and misdemeanour classes of offences and replaced them with an arrestable offence. Section 2(1) of the Act defines as an arrestable offence as *"an offence for which a person of full capacity and not previously convicted may, under or by virtue of any enactment, be punished by imprisonment for a term of five years or by a more severe penalty and includes an attempt to commit any such offence."*

Under this new class of offence a suspect can be arrested the same as for the old felony without a warrant.

Indictable and Summary Offences

Summary and indictable offences indicate the manner in which these offences are tried or dealt with in the courts. A summary (***relatively minor with the maximum sentence for one offence is 12 months***) offence is one which can only be dealt with by a judge sitting without a jury, (the District Court), while an indictable offence (***more serious offences which the jury decide the offenders' guilt***) is one which may be or must be tried before a judge and jury.

All common-law offences were held to be indictable offences as the common law did not distinguish or differentiate between indictable and non-indictable offences. However, criminal statutes or criminal laws passed into law by the Oireachtas (***all of the political parties and Seanad all working together***) do make a distinction between types of crimes and therefore differentiates on how different crimes will be dealt with by the courts.

When an offence is dealt with in a District Court, the judge is restricted in the length of sentence he/she can impose for any offence. **The Criminal Justice Act 1984 (Section11)** states that the maximum term of imprisonment that can be imposed by the District Court in respect of any number of offences for which sentence is passed at the same time cannot exceed 2 years. Similarly, the District Court cannot exceed a maximum sentence of 1 year in respect of one offence.

Examples of summary offences are:

Public Order Offence – Intoxication in a public place. The penalty for being found guilty of this offence is a class E fine. No imprisonment is available to the judge.

Public Order Offence- Threatening, abusive or insulting behaviour in a public place. The maximum penalty available to a judge where a person is found guilty of this offence is a class D fine or a term of imprisonment of up to three months or both a fine and a term of imprisonment.

Indictable offences tried summarily

Some offences are summarily offences, such as minor offences, other more serious such as theft and burglary are indictable (more serious) and the guilt or innocence of the suspect must be determined by a jury. However, there are "either way" offences which are indictable in nature but which under strict circumstances may be heard summarily by the judge alone, the condition of either way cases are:

1. The DPP must consent to a summary trial;
2. The District Court Judge must be satisfied that the offence is minor for the purposes of Article 38.2 of the Constitution.

Under s.2 of the Larceny Act 1916 a 3rd condition is imposed

3. The suspect must waive his right to a trial by jury.

Minor and non-minor offences

Article 38.2 of the Constitution of Ireland sets out those minor offences may be tried in courts of summary jurisdiction, that is, the District Courts. There is no definition of what a minor offence is in the Constitution although they are most often set down by the actual law. The distinction between the constitutional concepts of minor and non-minor offences equates more or less with the statutory distinction drawn between summary and indictable offences.

The Supreme Court has, however, considered the issue of what constitutes a minor offence. The most important case in this area is a case called **Melling v Ó Mathghamhna [1962] IR 1**. In examining the criteria or rules when deciding whether an offence was minor the Supreme Court laid out the following test:

- The severity or seriousness of the punishment
- Moral guilt of the suspect
- The law in 1937 when the Constitution was adopted, and
- Public opinion

The severity or seriousness of the punishment was the most important test

All that can be said with certainty is that an offence is minor where the punishment is less than six months imprisonment **(Conroy v Attorney General [1965] IR 411),** however, an offence is non-minor where the punishment is two years or more **(Mallon v Minister for Agriculture, Food and Forestry [1996] 1 IR 517).**

(**Example:** *Over time the courts have come to the belief that an offence with a maximum prison sentence of twelve months is considered a minor offence. It can be said as a result that any offence that carries a penalty of more than twelve months imprisonment is considered a non-minor offence or an indictable offence*)

An Introduction to Criminal Law in Ireland

Serious and non-serious offences

The Bail Act 1997, created a new distinction between serious and non-serious offences. The Act allows bail to be refused where a suspect is charged with a serious offence and it can be established that the suspect is likely to commit further serious offences if released on bail. **The Bail Act 1997** defines a serious offence as an offence for which a person, if convicted, could be imprisoned for 5 years or more.

Accomplice to Crime

Section 7(1) of the Criminal Law Act 1997, states that; any person who aids, abets, counsels or procures the commission of an indictable offence shall be liable to be indicted, tried and punished as a principal offender. In order to be tried as an accomplice the person need only know the nature or type of offence intended. So if a person knows that a theft of some sort is intended he will be liable for robbery if force was used. An accomplice may or may not be present when the crime is actually committed. However, without sharing the criminal intent, one who is merely present when a crime occurs and stands by silently is not an accomplice, no matter how reprehensible his or her inaction.

Some crimes are so defined that certain persons cannot be charged as accomplices even when their conduct significantly aids the chief offender.

Example, *if a person pays a blackmailer, who yields to the extortion demands of a racketeer, or a parent, who pays ransom to a kidnapper, may be unwise, but neither is a principal in the commission of the crimes.*

Even a victim may unwittingly create a perfect opportunity for the commission of a crime, but cannot be considered an accomplice because he or she lacks a criminal intent.

Principal in Crime

This was the actual person who commits the crime.

*(**Example**: The principle, say in a bank robbery, is the person who enters the bank and demands the money).*

An accomplice can also be charged as a principal, an accomplice is a person present at the commission of the crime who encourages or assists in its commission. Whether they aid or abet they are punished the same as the principle.

*(**Example:** A getaway driver does not actually go into the bank and demand money; however, they aid the principle in their crime by removing them from the scene)*

Accessory after the Fact

An accessory after the fact is a person who assists the principal to avoid detection, apprehension or conviction after the offence has been committed.

S. 7(2), Criminal Law Act, 1997 ('the 1997 Act') states, '*[w]here a person has committed an arrestable offence, any other person who, knowing or believing him...to be guilty of the offence or of some other arrestable offence, does without reasonable excuse any act with intent to impede his...apprehension or prosecution shall be guilty of an offence.*'

Differences between Crimes and Torts

There are distinct differences between crimes and torts.

Torts are actions taken against an individual (*or groups of individuals*) that are considered to have harmed that individual in some way (*emotional distress, etc.*) The person who was wronged "plaintiff" or "claimant" (*person bringing the claim*) sues the perpetrator "defendant" or "tortfeasor" (*person being sued*) and seeks financial restitution (*compensation*).

There can be some overlap between criminal and civil wrongs. For example, if a drunk driver crashes into the plaintiff's wall and damages it, the driver would be criminally liable for drink-driving is an offence under **S4 of the Road Traffic Act** and also the driver is also liable in tort for the damage to the plaintiff's wall and the plaintiff make a claim of the driver in a civil case to look for compensation.

Crimes are performing actions (*or inactions*) against the State that are considered to violate the written law and are, therefore, punishable by jail time, probation, and/or fines paid to the government.

Inchoate Offences

Incitement, Conspiracy and Attempt

Incitement, conspiracy and attempt are called "inchoate offences" because they criminalise conduct which may be described as working towards the commission of a particular offence.(*Inchoate Offences can be defined as unfinished offences*)

Attempt

Attempt crimes are crimes where the defendant's actions have the form of the actual committing of the crime itself: the actions must go beyond mere preparation.

The essence of the crime of attempt is that the defendant has failed to commit the Actus Reus ("guilty act") of the full offence, but has the direct and specific intent to commit that full offence. The normal rule for establishing criminal liability is to prove an Actus Reus accompanied by a Mens Rea ("guilty mind") at the relevant time (see concurrence and strict liability offences as the exception to the rule).

The People (Attorney General) v Sullivan [1964] IR 169, Walsh J stated - that charges of "attempts to commit statutory offences remain common law charges."

An Introduction to Criminal Law in Ireland

Public order offences in Ireland

The law on public order offences in Ireland is mainly set down in **the Criminal Justice (Public Order) Act, 1994**. This legislation deals with the behaviour of people in public places in Ireland and provides for various controls to be exercised at public events. The main purpose of the Act was as follows:

- To update the law in relation to public order offences;
- To create specific offences with regard to racketeering and demanding money with menaces;
- To deal with crowd control at public events; and
- To deal with miscellaneous (various) matters including a new offence prohibiting the advertising of brothels and prostitution.

For the purposes of the law in Ireland, a *'public place'* includes roads, public parks or recreational areas, cemeteries, churchyards, trains, buses and other public transport vehicles.

This Act gives the Gardaí the power to obtain from any offender their name and address, if asked, it is an offence not to give when asked under this Act their name and address, if they fail to give their name and address. The offender is liable on summary conviction to a class D fine for that offence.

The Criminal Justice (Public Order) Act 2003 provides that, if the offender is convicted of certain offences under the 1994 Act, the offender may be excluded from a premise for up to a year. This is in addition to the penalty under the 1994 Act.

Intoxication (being drunk) in a public place

Section 4 of the Criminal Justice (Public Order) Act 1994, deals with the offence of being intoxicated (*that is, drunk*) in a public place. While the maximum fine for being intoxicated in a public place in Ireland is a class E fine, the section gives the Gardaí the power to seize the intoxicating substance (*normally, alcohol or certain drugs*) where they suspect that an offence of being intoxicated in a public place is being committed.

Section 23(b) has been inserted in the Act by **section 184 of the Criminal Justice Act 2006** and provides for a fixed charge fine instead of court proceedings for being intoxicated in a public place. This fixed charge fine, currently €100, may be varied by the Minister for Justice and Equality. (Irish Statute Book, Criminal Justice Act 2006, 2010)

Disorderly conduct in a public place

This offence is concerned with what is described as "offensive conduct".

Section 5(i) of the Criminal Justice (Public Order) Act 1994 makes it an offence for anyone in a public place to engage in offensive conduct:

- Between the hours of 12 o'clock midnight and 7 o'clock in the morning next following; or

- At any time, after having been requested by a member of An Garda Siochana to desist.

Offensive conduct is unreasonable behaviour which (*having regard to the circumstances*), is likely to cause serious offence (or *serious annoyance)* to other people. The penalty for this offence is a class D fine.

Engaging in offensive conduct was introduced to deal with the types of disorderly behaviour which _fall short of threatening behaviour_ but could nevertheless adversely affect the quality of people's lives. A typical example of this offence would be people shouting late at night having left nightclubs, where this would cause serious annoyance to local residents. (DaveM)

Section 23(a) has been inserted in the Act by **Section 184 of the Criminal Justice Act 2006** and allows the Gardai to impose a fixed charge fine on any person for disorderly conduct in a public place instead of court proceedings. (*Pay a fine instead of going to court*) (Irish Statute Book, Criminal Justice Act 2006, 2010)

There is a provision for this fixed charge offence, the offender must give their name and address to the Garda. Failure to do so means they may be arrested without warrant and be convicted of a summary offence for which the maximum penalty is a class C fine. The Garda must serve the notice on the offender stating they will not be charged if they pay the fine within 28 days. The amount of the fixed charge, currently €140, is set by Regulations.

Threatening, abusive or insulting behaviour in a public place

***Section 6 of the Criminal Justice (Public Order) Act* 1994** makes it an offence for any person in a public place to use threatening, abusive or insulting words or behaviour with the intention of causing a breach of the peace.

Words or actions can be threatening, insulting or abusive if they were said in a way to entice a person into a fight, or where groups cause a fight to start when they use threatening words or actions.

Any person found guilty of this offence can be liable to class D fine and to a prison sentence of 3 months maximum.

Begging in an intimidating or threatening manner

Under ***Section 2 of the Criminal Justice (Public Order) Act 2011*** a person who begs in an aggressive, intimidating or aggressive manner is guilty of an offence. A person found guilty of such an offence is liable on summary conviction to a class E fine and/or up to one month in prison.

Section 2, covers situations such as someone begging next to an ATM, or bank etc., the begging itself is may not cause arrest, the arrest can happen when a person is directed by a Garda to move, and they refuse, or come back immediately.

This section also covers organised begging, such as gangs of beggars being dispersed in localities for the purpose of professional begging.

Distribution or display in a public place of material which is threatening, abusive, insulting or obscene

While ***Section 6 of the Criminal Justice (Public Order) Act 1994***, deals with words or behaviour. **Section 7,** of the 1994 Act, deals with distribution or display of offensive material. The courts will determine what is deemed offensive by using the reasonable person; they will ask if a reasonable person would deem that material offensive, obscene or insulting. This remains contentious as one person may deem it offensive yet others not.

Failure to comply with the direction of a member of An Garda Siochana

Section 8 of the Criminal Justice (Public Order) Act 1994 was designed to create an offence of failure to comply with a direction from a member of the Gardaí to desist (or stop) from conduct where the Garda has a reasonable apprehension (or fear) for the safety of persons or property or for the maintenance of the public peace. (Irish Statute Book, Criminal Justice (Public Order) Act, 1994, 2009)

It must be noted that the orders from the garda must be lawful, this is an area that needs further distinguished, for instance, if an officer was to instruct a driver which they had pulled over to put out their cigarette, this could cause some disagreement, i.e. is this a lawful request.

Example: *a driver has just been pulled over by the Gardaí. The driver is smoking a cigarette, this is a lawful activity, and smoking in your own car is lawful. The garda demands the driver extinguish his cigarette, so he can talk properly to the driver and the driver refuses, the garda gives the driver a fine because they refuse to comply with a garda direction, is this a lawful request?*

If the offender does not comply with a Garda's direction under this Act without lawful excuse is liable on summary conviction to a class D fine or to a maximum term of 6 months in prison or both.

Wilful obstruction

Section 9 of The Criminal Justice (Public Order) Act covers the offence of wilful obstruction of the highway. This offence is committed if a person, without lawful authority or excuse, in any way wilfully obstructs the free passage along a highway. This is to protect the citizen's constitutional right to free passage on any highway.

Entering a building, etc., with intent to commit an offence

Section 11 of the 1994 Act makes it an offence for anyone to enter (i.e. trespass) a building or the vicinity of a building with the intention of committing an offence and/or interfering with the property belonging to another. (Irish Statute Book, Criminal Justice (Public Order) Act, 1994, 2009)

Example, *the offender does not have to have entered the building to commit an offence under this section. Being on the property (i.e. in the back garden or the driveway of a house) will be enough to bring a person within the definition of this section. It will be a matter for the prosecution in any proceedings to prove that the suspect person was present in the building or on the property with the Mens Rea (intention) of committing an offence or with intent to interfere with the property. Those found guilty of this offence will be liable on summary conviction to a class C fine or to a maximum term in prison of 6 months or to both.*

Trespass on land /a building, etc.

Section 13 of the Criminal Justice (Public Order) Act 1994 covers Trespass to land, it is defined as: the intentional interference of one party, which directly interferes with the owner's exclusive possession of land. Land includes the actual soil/dirt, the structures/plants on it and the airspace above it

Under **Section 13,** the Gardaí may instruct an offender to desist where they fell that a person is trespassing and likely to cause fear to another person.

Where one party physical interference which disturbs the owners exclusive possession of the land the Gardaí may direction them to leave, if they refuse

without lawful excuse or reason, they will be guilty of an offence and is liable to a fine or imprisonment or both. However, the owner must prove that they have <u>exclusive possession</u> of the land at the time of the interference with the <u>exclusion of all others.</u> This does not mean they have to own the land; Ownership refers to *title* in the land. Exclusive possession refers to *physical* holding of the land

Riot

The offence of riot is seen as one of the major and most serious of the public order offences. ***Section 14 of the Criminal Justice (Public Order) Act 1994*** defines riot as; (Irish Statute Book S14)

"Where – 12 or more persons who are present together at any place (public or private) use or threaten to use ***unlawful violence for a common purpose***,

Firstly there's a factual number requirement. There have to be at least 12 people. Secondly they have to be present together. Thirdly they have to use or threaten unlawful violence so it's not all of them have to be using it. Now the violence has to be threatened for a common purpose. Common purpose must be present, but it can be difficult, to define in layman's terms, (the Gardaí will define if "all of the 12" intended violence) for instance, if there are 6 people pro and 6 people anti… what happens here, they have two different objectives in common, but is that common intent it to fight…?? So is there 6 people and 6 people with opposing view and intentions, or 12 people intending to fight, this can be a little difficult to define and each incident must be taken into account by the Gardaí present to decide.

Gardaí can use Riot in situations where large groups assemble in protest and the protest turns into unlawful violence. The maximum penalty for the offence of riot is an unlimited fine and/or a period of imprisonment for up to ten years.

Violent disorder

Violent disorder, which is covered by ***Section 15 of the Act***, is similar to the offence of riot although it is a lesser version of that offence. Violent disorder reduces the number of ***persons present to a minimum of three***. These persons present must use or threaten to use violence and the conduct of those persons, taken together is such as would cause a person of reasonable firmness, if present at that place, to fear for his or her safety or the safety of another person. (Irish Statute Book S15, 2012)

For an offence of riot to take place the suspect person must have used violence whereas in the case of violent disorder the suspect person need only threaten to use violence. N.B. riot and violent disorder differ in that there is no requirement for the group to share a common design or purpose. The maximum penalty for violent disorder is an unlimited fine and or a period of imprisonment for up to ten years.

Affray

Section 16 of the Criminal Justice (Public Order) Act 1994 states- "Where –

Two or more persons at any place (public or private) use or threaten to use violence towards each other, and the violence so used or threatened by one of those persons is unlawful.

Firstly, there only has to be two persons, the key thing this person has to do is use or threaten unlawful violence. What's different though between riot, violent disorder and affray is this. In riot or violent disorder using or threatening unlawful violence was sufficient.

In order to prove affray it must be proved that the use or threat of unlawful violence is directed towards another ACTUAL person, **the violence involved in affray must be directed towards each other and not innocent bystanders**... It can't be a face in the crowd. It has to be directed towards a specific person.

*An **example** of this would simply be a group of persons fighting against each other in the street. Also with the other two offences, the **affray can take place in public or in private**. A person convicted of affray may receive a maximum penalty of an unlimited fine and or a term of imprisonment for up to five years.*

Blackmail, extortion and demanding money with menaces

Section 17 of the Criminal Justice (Public Order) Act 1994 creates a new version of the blackmail and extortion offences which were previously contained in ***the Larceny Act, 1916*** these are now ***repealed*** (*removed/deleted*). If a person makes an unjustified demand with menaces, (*they will be making a gain for themselves or another or with the intention to cause a loss to another*), they will be guilty of this offence. The exception to this offence is that if the person making the demand with menaces believes that:-

- He has reasonable grounds for making the demand, and
- The use of menaces is a proper means of reinforcing the demand.

The act itself does not define the word "menaces" the meaning of the word was defined in case-law under **the Old Larceny Act, 1916**.

In a case called **Thorne–v-Motor Trade Association (1937)[1]** in this case the court stated that:-"*the word menace is to be liberally construed, and not as limited to threats of violence but as to include threats of any action detrimental to or unpleasant to the person addressed*". (Elawresources, 2009)

Example, *if A owes B money, they ask them to repay the debt, by instalments or by lump sum, this is a legitimate debt and legitimate demand for repayment, however, say if A was to threaten to post on the internet details of a person's sexual life or threats to publish explicit photographs of a person. If those threats are made it negates the legitimate demand for the payment of the debt.*

If a person is convicted of this offence the maximum punishment is an unlimited fine and/or a term of imprisonment of up to 14 years.

Assault with intent to cause bodily harm or commit an indictable offence

While the main area of law that deals with assault is the **Non-fatal Offences against the Person Act, 1997**, **Section 18 of the Criminal Justice (Public Order) Act 1994** (Irish Statute book, 2009) creates an additional offence of assault with intent to cause bodily harm or to commit an indictable offence. This is an aggravated assault and states-

---

[1] Thorne v Motor Trade Association [1937] AC 797. Lord Wright: "I think the word 'menace' is to be liberally construed and not as limited to threats of violence but as including threats of any action detrimental to or unpleasant to the person addressed. It may also include a warning that in certain events such action is intended."

"Any person who assaults another person with intent to cause bodily harm or to commit an indictable offence shall be guilty of an offence".

Where a person is convicted of this offence they could face a maximum penalty of an unlimited fine and or imprisonment of up to five years.

Assault or obstruction of a peace officer

Section 19 of the Criminal Justice (Public Order) Act 1994 defines a *"Peace Officer"* as a member of the Garda Siochana, a Prison Officer or a member of the Defence Forces. (Section 185 of the Criminal Justice Act, 2012), has extended this definition to include ambulance personnel and fire brigade personnel. The offence replaces the old offence of assaulting or obstructing a peace officer which was contained in *section 38 of the Offences against the Person Act, 1861.* The important elements of this offence are as follows:

- That the assault was on a peace officer acting in the execution of their duty, or
- That the assault was on any other person who was aiding or assisting the peace officer, or
- That the assault on any other person was to prevent the lawful arrest or detention of himself or of any other person for any offence.

Likewise, where a person wilfully obstructs Gardaí acting in the course of their duty or obstructs any person who is assisting or helping the peace office in the course of their duty, they will also be guilty of the offence. N.B, the offender is given a choice as to whether or not to have their case dealt with in the District Court or to have the case dealt with in the Circuit Criminal Court before a jury. (***Indictable offence tried Summary***)

If someone is convicted in the District Court the maximum penalty is a class A fine and/or a term of imprisonment not exceeding 12 months. In relation to obstruction, the maximum penalty is a class C fine and/or a term of imprisonment of 6 months.

Attacks on emergency service personnel

The Criminal Justice Act 2006 has, as mentioned above, amended ***Section 19 of the Criminal Justice (Public Order) Act 1994*** to include people providing emergency services. The Act creates new offences of assaulting or obstructing emergency service personnel, such as fire brigade personnel and ambulance crews, engaged in providing emergency services. It also covers those working in accident and emergency departments of hospitals. (Citizen Information, 2011)

Chapter 2

The Criminal Court System, Arrest and Detention

- summarise the functions of the Gardaí, Courts, Prison Service, Probation Service and Director of Public Prosecutions in the Criminal Justice System
- demonstrate an understanding of the Criminal Court System outlining in detail the five main courts
- outline the procedure for taking a person before a court on a criminal charge
- outline the law in relation to bail; understanding the system in place in Ireland
- refer to rights of silence and presumption of innocence
- define arrest and outline the powers provided to Gardaí at common law
- understand the relevant legislation governing arrest, define arrestable offence under **the Criminal Law Act 1997**
- explanation of detention; outline **section 30 of the Offences Against The State Act 1939** clearly illustrating the circumstances under which detention may be extended
- outline **Section 4 of the Criminal Justice Act 1984**
- explain and give examples of drug offences, refer to **section 2 of the Drug Trafficking Act 1996**.

Court Structure In Ireland (below)

THE STRUCTURE OF IRISH COURTS

There are other administrative courts such as the Employment Appeals Tribunal, An Bord Pleanála, and the Labour Court inside the court hierarchy and structure.

The Courts and Court Officers (Amendment) Act 2007 states the numbers of judges in the District court, 63, Circuit, 37, High 37, Special, 11 (from a panel), 3, 5 or 7 in the Supreme Court.

Supreme Court

Final Court of Appeal (in cases of Fact only) only hears appeals, this court is not a court of first instance, (it never hears a case for the first time). It deals with matters of law or procedure where it's of national interest for the country such as the constitutionality of any legislation which may be referred under Article 26 of the constitution. The Supreme Court can determine or question capacity of the President. Three (ordinarily) or five (national importance) or 7 (Article 26) judges sit. Decisions made based on majority ruling, although each judge is eligible to provide a separate judgement, whether or not it agrees with majority rulings.

Court of Criminal Appeal

This court deals with appeals, persons convicted on impeachment in Circuit Court, Central Criminal Court or Special Criminal Court.

Special Criminal Court

This court deals with criminal charges relating to terrorist organizations and organized drug activities. Brought into being to secure effective administration of justice, preservation of public peace. It consists of three judges sitting without a jury. Set up under the *Offences against the State Act 1939*

Central Criminal Court

The Central Criminal Court is the criminal section of the High Court, it deals with serious indictable offences,. these would include rape, murder, piracy and treason.

Court of Civil Appeal

Hears appeals from High Court except cases where Supreme Court permits appeals. Gives ruling on question of law acquiesced to it by, Circuit Courts. It hears appeals from cases heard in High Court about whether or not a law is constitutional.

High Court

The High Court has *full original jurisdiction (it can hear any case from anywhere for any amount)* in authority to determine, all complications, whether law or fact, civil and criminal. It has the authority to determine the validity of any law which is referred to it from the president under Article 26 of the constitution. It also deals with separation and divorce cases.

Circuit Court

The Circuit Civil Court deals with cases from €15k to €75k (Contract) and €60k (Tort) it also deals with family law separations and divorce.

The circuit criminal court deals with indictable offences which are less serious, i.e. theft burglary robbery, some less indictable offences can be tried summarily in the district court with permission from the accused, DPP and the Judge. In criminal cases the judge sits with a jury. This court can also hear appeals from the District Court

Commercial Court

Provides efficient, effective dispute resolution in commercial cases greater than €1 million. Disputes concern of large commercial properties. Appeals or application for judicial review of regulator decisions.

District Court

The district civil court deals with minor civil law cases, maintenance orders up to €150.00, minor tort cases, this judge has the jurisdiction to deal with cases up to €15,000. this can deal with appeals from employment tribunals.

The district criminal court deals with minor offences, and offences which will give minor fines, in the district court you the maximum fine is €1905 and you will get a maximum sentence of 12 months for one offence and 24 months for two or more offences. This court deals with summary offences (less serious). Judge, no jury.

Small Claims

Claims up to €2k are dealt with without the need for a solicitor. The District Court Registrar will process the claim. S/he will try to reach a settlement if this is not possible it will be brought before the District Court.

Jurisdiction means; what the court has the power to deal with. i.e limited jurisdiction in the district court is €15,000, local jurisdiction in the district civil court is where the defendant lives or where the tort or contract took place. Original jurisdiction means a case from any area for any amount.

A summary offence is a minor offence heard by a judge only. Indictable is a more serious offence which is heard by judge and jury

An Introduction to Criminal Law in Ireland

The functions of the Gardaí

The primary function of An Garda Síochána is to ensure that people feel safe on the streets and in their homes. Building stronger and safer communities contributes greatly to improving the quality of life for the people.

The function of An Garda Síochána is to serve the community by implementing and upholding the law as legislated by Government. With the participation and dedication of the Gardaí, other community stakeholders (e.g. retail outlets, public services, public amenities) are, as far as possible, ensured of safety, and they in turn commit to law abidance to serve the common good of the community. To ensure a positive strategy, issues such as the quality of the service provided and the strength and commitment of the partnerships amongst service providers and citizens must be ensured.

The Gardaí make a commitment to the community they serve, to provide:

- a good quality service,
- an open and transparent force which is accountable for its actions,
- the equal provision of services towards all members of the community who access the service or come into contact with the force,
- consultation and information to the local community on issues that impact them or may do so in the future and
- support to the local community activities by playing an active role.

The Function of the Courts

The courts' system in Ireland has its historic origins in the British Courts System that was in use in Ireland up to 1922. The 1922 Constitution was enacted on the foundation of the Irish Free State. That Constitution provided for the setting up of new courts to replace the existing Courts that had evolved under the British administration. ***The Courts of Justice Act, 1924*** established the legal basis for a new Court system.

Ireland has a written Constitution and Articles 34 to 37 of the Constitution deal with the administration of justice in general. Article 34.1 states that 'Justice shall be administered in Courts established by law'.

The Constitution outlines the structure of the court system as comprising:

- A court of final appeal, known as the Supreme Court,

- Courts of first instance which include the High Court with full jurisdiction in all criminal and civil matters and
- Courts of limited jurisdiction including
- the Circuit Court and the
- District Court organised on a regional basis.

The present courts were set up by **the Courts (Establishment and Constitution) Act 1961** pursuant to Article 34 of the Constitution adopted by the Irish people in 1937. We are concerned mainly with the courts as they are relevant to personal injury and property litigation, and we have focused on this area in the linked pages attached.

The Courts Act 2004 contains much that is relevant to the day-to-day handling of Personal Injury Claims within the Courts System.

- District Court
- Circuit Court
- High Court
- Central Criminal Court
- Appeal Court
- Supreme Court
- Courts Act 2004

An Introduction to the Irish Court System

The Irish Court system was established under Articles 64 to 73 of the Irish Constitution enacted in 1922. **The Courts of Justice Act 1924** set out the structure and Hierarchy of the Irish Courts and the final structure of the Irish Courts was set out in the Irish Constitution of 1937 under Articles 34 to 38, there was a Constitutional challenge to the structure and hierarchy of the Courts set out in the 1937 Constitution, this challenge case *"The State (Killian) v Minister for Justice [1954]"*[2] found that new legislation was required to re-establish the hierarchy and structure of the Courts. This legislation came in the form of **the Courts (Establishment and Constitution) Act 1961 and the Courts (Supplemental Provisions) Act 1961.**

---

[2] The State (Killian) v Minister for Justice [1954] IR 207

Article 34 of the Irish Constitution states that: *"Justice shall be administered in courts established by law by Judges appointed in the manner provided by this Constitution"*[3] *"justice will be administered by courts established by law and justice should generally be administered in public"*. This does not cover family law

Article 38 of the Irish Constitution states that 'no person shall be tried on any criminal charge save in the due course of law'.

The Irish Court system is hierarchical in nature with the Supreme Court being the highest, followed by the High Court, the Circuit Court, and the District Court. The Employment Appeals Tribunal, An Bord Pleanála, and the Labour Court are in the administrative divisions and deal with specialised areas of the law.

The superiority of Supreme Court judges was set out in *the Courts of Justice Act 1924* and confirmed by *the Courts Act 1997.*

The Hierarchy of the Courts, starting with the inferior courts are as follows:

The District Court in Ireland

The District Court is the lowest court in the court system; the District Court was established in 1961. *The Courts and Court Officers (Amendment) Act 2007* the numbers of judges should not be more than 60, excluding the President of the Court, however this has since been extended to 63. The currently President is Judge Rosemary Horgan.

There are 24 Districts in Ireland, including the Dublin Metropolitan District, each with its own court being presided over by a judge sitting alone (that is, one judge, no jury).

<u>Function & Jurisdiction</u>

The District Court hears civil and criminal which are relatively minor. The District Court hear cases which are Summary in nature

---

[3]http://www.supremecourt.ie/supremecourt/sclibrary3.nsf/pagecurrent/D5F78352A387D74480 257315005A419E?opendocument&l=en

District Civil Court

In civil cases, its monetary jurisdiction is limited to €15,000, meaning that that is the maximum award a judge can make in respect of a civil case. These cases are usually in Contract or Tort. It has the jurisdiction to grant liquor and lottery and competition licences, and can hear certain family matters, including issues relating to maintenance, which is limited to €150 per week per child, and €500 per week in respect of a spouse, access and guardianship, and can grant Safety Orders and Barring Orders, issues pursuant to the Control of Dogs Acts, applications to have birth and marriage certificates amended and applications for noise reduction orders under the ***Environmental Protection Act 1992***.

District Criminal Court

In criminal matters, its jurisdiction is limited to cases which a judge sits alone, (there is no jury) the maximum penalty is 12 months' imprisonment for one offence or 24 months for two or more offences. Again, the maximum penalty is 12 months' imprisonment for one offence or 24 months for two or more offences. Cases in the District Court are those that are non-jury trials of minor offences which include most road traffic offences, TV licensing offences and parking fines, these are called Summary (or less serious) offences.

There are some Indictable (more serious) cases that cannot be heard in the District Court, including, rape, treason, murder, aggravated sexual assault, and piracy, which can never be heard in the District Court and must be referred up to the Circuit Court or the Central Criminal Court.

In respect of offences, the District Court Judge will be presented with the Book of Evidence, the prosecution and defence will present their submissions including bail applications, before deciding whether there is a sufficient case to answer. If so, the suspects will be sent forward for trial to the Circuit Court or the Central Criminal Court, depending on the severity of the offence.

Appeals

There are, essentially, two types of appeal: a *de novo* appeal, and an appeal on a point of law.

De novo

When a *de novo* appeal is granted it means that the case is completely re-heard from the beginning by a higher court. For District Court cases, all *de novo* appeals are heard by the Circuit Court. The Circuit Court's determination is final and cannot be appealed.

On a point of law

These are heard by the High Court, and can occur either during the case (referred to as a "consultative case stated") or after the case has been heard in full (referred to as "an appeal by way of case stated"). In such appeals, the High Court is only concerned with the legal issues and not in the findings of the District Court.

An example of this would be where there was some confusion as to the meaning of a particular law (legislation). If this was the case, the matter could be sent to the High Court to clear up any ambiguity. Once the matter is cleared up it is sent back to the District Court so that the case may continue, or so that any relevant changes can be made to the ruling.

Judicial review

While not strictly an appeal, there is also a remedy called *judicial review.* In the District Court, this means that, where an individual is of the belief that a judge or other government agency has acted in excess of its jurisdiction (*Ultra Virus*) or contrary to its duty, that person can query or challenge that action in the High Court.

The Small Claims Court

The small claims court deals mainly with minor matters. It provides consumers with an inexpensive and fast way to resolve disputes. This court is dealt with through the District Court offices.

The Maximum claim that can be brought in the Small Claims court is €2.000 and normally deals with consumer matters and occasional small business complaints. Consumer claims such as faulty goods or bad workmanship are the normal type of consumer cases brought by persons in the small claims court. To be a consumer you must have bought the goods or engaged the service for private use from someone who sells them in the course of business.

You may also claim for the non-return of a rent deposit for some kinds of rented properties, such as a holiday home but excluded are deposit claims for private residential accommodation. Claims cannot be made in the Small Claims Court for debts, personal injuries or breach of leasing or hire-purchase agreements.

The procedure for making a claim is commenced by lodging the claim with the District Court Registrar, and paying the fee of €25.00. The other party (respondent or the person being claimed against) will then be notified by the registrar of the District Court. If the Respondent does not agree with the claim they can dispute it by giving notice to the Registrar who will attempt to settle the claim, failing this case is set down for hearing. The case will be heard by a District Court Judge.

The parties can appeal the decision in the case to the Circuit Court within 14 days of the court hearing. If the decision is being appealed, the parties should consider obtaining legal advice.

An Introduction to Criminal Law in Ireland

The Circuit Court in Ireland

Under *the Court and Court Officers (Amendment) Act 2007* the Circuit Court consists of 37 ordinary judges and is presided over by Mr. Justice Raymond Groarke.

There are 8 Circuits in Ireland – Dublin, Cork, Eastern, South Eastern, Western, South Western, Northern, and Midlands. Dublin and Cork are the only permanent courts throughout the year. There are 10 judges assigned to the Dublin Circuit Court, and 3 to the Cork Circuit Court, the rest are divided between the remaining Circuit Courts. It also acts as an appeal court from the District Court. In criminal cases the Circuit Court is presided over by a judge sitting with a jury of twelve persons. In civil cases the Court is presided over by a judge sitting alone.

Function & Jurisdiction of the Circuit Court

The Circuit Court hears civil and criminal cases in a variety of matters which also include de novo appeals from the District Court. The Circuit Court covers indictable offences and has a jury

Structure of the Circuit Civil Court

The monetary jurisdiction in the Circuit Court is currently limited to where the claim does not exceed €75,000.00 and personal injury cases where the claim does not exceed €60,000, this means that that is the maximum monetary award that a judge can award when hearing a civil case. The Circuit Court deals with all breach of contract, property damage cases, family law i.e. judicial separation, divorce, nullity, and all ancillary matters i.e. family law matters which can have secondary awards such as property division, land division, legal fees etc.

Structure of the Circuit Criminal Court

The Circuit Court has a wide jurisdiction in respect of criminal matters. It deals with all indictable offences which are sent forward from the District Court, however there are some exceptions, including rape, murder, aggravated sexual assault, treason, and piracy. These cases must be heard in the Central Criminal Court.

Appeals

Apart from hearing appeals from the District Court, the Circuit Court can also hear appeals from decisions of the Labour Court, the Unfair Dismissals Tribunal, and the Employment Appeals Tribunal. There are in essence two types of appeal available to those whose judgements are in the Circuit Court: a *de novo* appeal, and an appeal on a point of law.

De novo

When a *de novo* appeal is granted it means that the case is completely re-heard from the beginning by a higher court. For District Court cases, all *de novo* appeals are heard by the High Court. For criminal cases, all *de novo* appeals are heard by the Court of Criminal Appeal. Determinations of the High Court and the Court of Criminal Appeal are final and cannot be appealed.

On a point of law

These are heard by the High Court, and can occur either during the case (referred to as a "consultative case stated") or after the case has been heard in full (referred to as "an appeal by way of case stated"). In such appeals, the High Court is only concerned with the legal issues and not in the findings of the Circuit Court. An example of this would be where there was some confusion as to the meaning of a particular law (legislation). If this was the case, the matter could be sent to the High Court to clear up any ambiguity. Once the matter is cleared up it is sent back to the Circuit Court so that the case may continue, or so that any relevant changes can be made to the ruling.

Judicial review

While not strictly an appeal, there is also a remedy called **judicial review.** In the Circuit Court, this means that, where an individual is of the belief that a judge or other government agency has acted in excess of its jurisdiction (**Ultra Virus**) or contrary to its duty, that person can query or challenge that action in the High Court.

Circuit Court, County Registrar's duties and Responsibilities

The Registrar is also responsible for Motions of Discovery or issues arising in the service of documents.

The High Court in Ireland

The High Court of Ireland has full original jurisdiction the power "to determine all matters and questions whether of law or fact, civil or criminal". It can decide the validity of any law, having regard to the provisions of the Constitution and hear murder and rape trials though under **Competition Act, 2002** and associated cases or cases that results from it.

Structure of the High Court of Ireland

The High Court is presided over by the Honourable Mr. Justice Nicholas Kearns and 36 ordinary judges. In Civil cases one judge sitting alone usually presides over the proceedings, but in some cases of defamation, assault and battery, false imprisonment, and malicious prosecution all require a jury. There are times for instance when there is a case of national importance i.e. the constitutionality of a new bill, the High Court will sit with three judges. The High Court hears appeals from the Circuit Court in civil cases. There are no juries per se in civil cases in the High Court with one exception; this exception is in libel cases where the case will be decided by a judge and jury.

The High Court is based in Dublin but a division of the High Court sits in several provincial locations such as Cork, Galway, Limerick, Waterford, Sligo, Dundalk, Kilkenny and Ennis at specified times during the year to deal with personal injury cases and appeals from the various Circuit Courts in civil and family law matters.

Function & Jurisdiction of the High Court of Ireland

The High Court has full original jurisdiction, there is no local or limited jurisdiction. It can hear any cases for any amounts.

The High Court also hears de novo appeals from the Circuit Court in civil matters and appeals on a point of law from the District Court.

Structure of the High Court of Ireland

The High Court of Ireland also hears a variety of commercial issues, including applications to wind up a company, and bankruptcy matters. Other common types of cases to come before the High Court include personal injuries, defamation, and contract cases. Further, the High Court can hear judicial review applications in respect of government bodies, various tribunals, and even decisions of lower courts.

On the whole although the High Court can hear any case as it has original jurisdiction claims of over €75,000 (€65,000 in tort) are usually dealt with in the High court, this has to do with practicalities and costs.

Structure of the High Court (Central Criminal Court) of Ireland

Where criminal matters are concerned, the High Court is referred to as the Central Criminal Court, or the Criminal Court area of the High Court. This court only hears cases of a more serious nature which the lower courts cannot deal with lower courts. Examples include murder, rape, aggravated sexual assault, treason, and piracy.

Appeals in the High Court of Ireland

An appeal from the High Court in civil cases can only go to the Supreme Court on foot of permission which is applied for under the "leapfrog appeal" system, however all other appeals go to the Court of Appeal..

Master of the High Court

The administrator of the High Court is the Master, their role is similar to that of the County Registrar of the Circuit Court, in that he is authorised to deal with various administrative matters in civil cases.

The Special Criminal Court in Ireland

Deals with:

- treason
- encouragement or concealing knowledge of treason
- offences relating to the obstruction of government and obstruction of the President
- murder, attempted murder, conspiracy to murder
- piracy
- offences under the Genocide Act, 1973
- rape, aggravated sexual assault and attempted aggravated sexual assault under the Criminal Law (Rape) (Amendment) Act, 1990

The Special Criminal Court was set up under **the Offences against the State Act 1939** and sits with no jury. The cases it can deal with are limited and usually Terrorism or Gangland.

There is no Jury in this court and is presided over by three judges, these three judges are taken from a pool of 11 judges which are chosen from the High, Circuit and District Courts. Appeals from the Special Criminal Court against conviction or sentence are taken to the Court of Appeal.

The Court of Appeal in Ireland

The Court of Appeal, came into existence on 28th October 2014, it was established by the **Court of Appeal Act 2014,** the Court of Appeal which sits between the High Court and the Supreme Court.

The Court of Appeal is composed of a President and nine ordinary judges. The Chief Justice and the President of the High Court (The Honourable Mr Justice Sean Ryan) in addition to the President, the Court will comprise nine ordinary judges. Six High Court judges have been nominated for appointment to the Court, namely Mr Justice Peter Kelly, Ms Justice Mary Finlay Geoghegan, Mr Justice George Birmingham, Ms Justice Mary Irvine, Mr Justice Gerard Hogan, and, Mr Justice Michael Peart. The remaining three positions have yet to be filled by the Judicial Appointments Advisory Board.

Some interlocutory and procedural applications may be heard by the President alone or by another judge nominated by the President. The Court of Appeal will be an automatic appeal court from the High

Appeals in civil proceedings

The Court has jurisdiction to hear appeals in civil proceedings from the High Court which would have been heard by the Supreme Court prior to the introduction of the Court of Civil Appeal.

It is possible to bypass the Court of Appeal or 'Leap Frog' an appeal to the Supreme Court., however permission from the Supreme Court to bring a Leapfrog Appeal must be obtained, this is not an automatic entitlement and will only be granted if the Supreme Court is satisfied that (i) the High Court decision involves a matter of general public importance; and/or (ii) the interests of justice require that the appeal be heard by the Supreme Court.[4]

The Court can hear appeals from cases heard in the High Court about whether or not a law is constitutional. The Constitution provides that no laws may be passed restricting the Court of Appeal's jurisdiction to do this.

---

[4] http://www.arthurcox.com/wp-content/uploads/2014/09/Arthur-Cox-Irelands-New-Court-of-Appeal-September-2014.pdf

Appeals in criminal proceedings

Under **the Court of Appeal Act 2014**, the Court of Appeal was given the appellate jurisdiction previously exercised by the Court of Criminal Appeal.

Criminal Appeals from the Circuit Court or Central Criminal Court who require a certificate from the trial judge that the case is a fit one for appeal now lie to the Court of Appeal. If this certificate is refused, the Court of Appeal itself, on appeal from this refusal, can grant leave to appeal. In addition, the Director of Public Prosecutions may appeal a sentence on grounds of alleged undue leniency under section 2 of the **Criminal Justice Act 1993**. An alleged case under miscarriage of justice, an appeal can be lodged under section 2 of the **Criminal Procedure Act 1993**. [5]

The Court of Appeal was also given jurisdiction to hear appeals by the Director of Public Prosecutions on a question of law arising out of criminal trials which resulted in an acquittal. The decision of the Court of Appeal does not affect the acquittal verdict in such cases.

Appeals by the Director of Public Prosecutions against an acquittal or against a decision not to order a retrial also lie to the Court of Appeal.

Courts-Martial appeals

Under the **Court of Appeal Act 2014**, the Court of Appeal was given the appellate jurisdiction previously exercised by the Courts-Martial Appeal Court. This means that appeals from people who have been convicted by a court-martial now lie to the Court of Appeal.

Cases stated

Questions of law which could previously be referred by the Circuit Court to the Supreme Court for determination (a 'case stated') are now determinable by the Court of Appeal.

---

[5]http://www.courts.ie/Courts.ie/library3.nsf/pagecurrent/5E9C21E72309A7D280257D7F0045A86A?opendocument

Appealing decisions of the Court of Appeal

Unless under very limited circumstances all decisions in the Court of Appeal are final, except in the following limited circumstances whereby permission can be sought from the Supreme Court to hear an appeal under **Article 34.5.3 of the Constitution** where:

(i)   the decision of the Court of Appeal involves a matter of general public importance;

and/ or

(ii)   (ii) the interests of justice require that a further appeal be heard by it.

The Supreme Court in Ireland

The Supreme Court sits in the Four Courts in Dublin and is the highest court in the system. It consists of the President or the Chief Justice, her Honour Ms. Justice Susan Denham and 7 ordinary judges. Under **section.5 of the Courts (No. 2) Act 1997**, the number of judges may also be exceeded by one where a former Chief Justice serves as a judge of the Supreme Court. The Court hears appeals from the High Court and the Court of Appeal. The Court has the power to decide if the provisions of any statute are repugnant to the Constitution should the President refer such provisions to the Court prior to the statute being enacted. Under **Article 26 of the Irish Constitution 1937** the President has the power to send a Bill to the Supreme Court to test its constitutionality before signing it into law

In procedural matters or minor cases, three judges sit. For matters involving a constitutional challenge to a statute, or where an important question of law arises, five judges' sit, the Supreme Court can be requested to review a Bill referred to it by the President as to whether or not such a Bill is repugnant to the Constitution, if this event takes place then seven judges sit. Where there are applications for the appointment of Notaries Public and Commissioners for Oaths, or for case management lists the Chief Justice can sit alone.

Appeals

The main day-to-day business of the Supreme Court is to hear appeals from the Court of Appeal, or from the High Court ("leapfrog" appeals under limited circumstances "see high court notes").

The Supreme Court does not hear the evidence of witnesses as there is no witness box in the Supreme Court. Appeals are heard on the basis of the documents that were before the original court and a transcript of the oral evidence that was given in the original court and, where the trial judge approves them, legal counsels' notes of the evidence.

Decisions of Judges in the Supreme Court

Decisions are made based on a majority ruling, though each judge is entitled to deliver a separate judgement, regardless of whether or not it agrees with the majority ruling. There are two exceptions to this – where deciding on the validity of a law or on the constitutionality or otherwise of a Bill, the majority decision is the only one pronounced.

These decisions are sometimes given ex tempore (immediately). There are times however when Judges reserve the right to reserve its decision pending consideration of the facts whereby they will deliver their decision at a future date.

The Children's Court

The structure of the Children Court is much different to that of the adult courts, firstly, there is no jury both summarily and indictable offences are tried by a judge only and in camera (not in the public eye, i.e. private) It also differs in that the young offenders are given breaks and their case is dealt with quickly in order that they are not "hanging around"

- The Court does not have jurisdiction over all cases. Serious indictable offences are to be referred to the Central Criminal Court.

The Children's Court however will not deal with serious offences such as rape, murder etc., these have to be dealt with in the adult courts, including the public and media attention which comes with these cases.

An Introduction to Criminal Law in Ireland

Personnel involved in the court room

The Judge

The judge is in charge of court proceedings and decides any legal issues arising in the case.

The Registrar / Court Clerk

The registrar / court clerk assists the judge with administrative matters and is in charge of the court documents and exhibits. He/she also records the names of witnesses and the decision in the case. The registrar / court clerk also administers the oath.

Solicitor

Solicitors meet with clients and get instructions from them. They prepare the case for trial by getting the papers ready and choosing/briefing a barrister to present the case.

The Jury

The jury hears the evidence and decides on the guilt or innocence of the suspect in a criminal case and which party wins in a civil case.

The Court Reporter / Stenographer

The stenographer takes a note of everything said in the case and later types up the notes in the event of an appeal being lodged.

Witness

Witnesses are called by either party to prove their side of the story and may be cross-examined by the opposing party as to the accuracy of their evidence.

Counsel

The barristers in the case are known as counsel. They are hired by the solicitor to prosecute or defend the case in court.

An Introduction to Criminal Law in Ireland

DPP (criminal)

The Department of public prosecutions brings cases against the suspect in criminal cases, they bring the case on behalf of the citizens.

Tipstaff / Judge's Usher

The tipstaff / judge's usher is the personal assistant to the judge. He/she walks ahead of the judge carrying a staff and says "all rise" as the judge enters the courtroom.

Defendant (criminal)

The suspect comes before the court suspect of a crime.

Defendant (civil)

The person being sued or the case is being brought against.

Plaintiff

The person bringing the civil case against another civilian or the state.

Prison Officer (Criminal)

Sits in attendance with the suspect.

Public

Members of the general public are permitted in the public gallery, except in camera or family/child custody cases.

Civil Liability & Courts Act 2004

Many people involved in claims believe that over time this act has an even greater chance of revolutionising the overall scene. While no one has objection to reasonable compensation being paid to genuine claimants by those who are liable for their injuries, far too often many of these vital components were ignored. Added to this was the requirement to pay costs in far too many straightforward cases. PIAB is really more about that problem, The Courts Act begins to get to the heart of the matter.

The Irish Prison Service

Political responsibility for the Prison System in Ireland is vested in the Minister for Justice and Equality. The Irish Prison Service operates as an executive agency within the Department of Justice and Equality. It is headed by a Director General supported by 7 Directors. The Irish Prison Service is administered centrally with its headquarters located at IDA Business Park, Ballinalee Road, Longford, Co. Longford

The Prison Service operates within a statutory framework comprising:

(i) the Prisons Acts, including the most recent **Prisons Act 2007,**

(ii) relevant provisions in other statutes such as **the Prisons (Visiting Committees) Act, 1925, the Criminal Justice Act, 1960, the Criminal Justice (Miscellaneous Provisions) Act, 1997, the Criminal Justice Act, 2007, other criminal justice acts and the Transfer of Sentenced Persons Acts, 1995 and 1997** and

(iii) **the Rules for the Government of Prisons, 2007.**

For persons held on immigration related matters the main legislative provisions are the Immigration Acts 1999, 2003 and 2004, their associated regulations, the Illegal Immigrants Trafficking Act 2000 and the Refugee Act 1996.

The Prison Service also takes due account of the UN and European Conventions on Human Rights, UN Standard Minimum Rules for the Treatment of Prisoners, the UN Convention against Torture and other Cruel, Inhuman or Degrading Treatment or Punishment, the UN Covenant on Civil and Political Rights, the European Convention for the Prevention of Torture and Inhuman or Degrading Treatment or Punishment.

Location of Prisons and Places of Detention

Ireland's Prisons

There are 14 institutions in the Irish Prison System consisting of 11 traditional "closed" institutions, two open centres which operate with minimal internal and perimeter security, and one "semi-open" facility with traditional perimeter security but minimal internal security (the Training Unit). The majority of female prisoners are accommodated in the purpose-built "Dóchas Centre" and the remainder are located in a separate part of Limerick Prison.

Mountjoy	Committal prison for adult male prisoners, at North Circular Road, Dublin 7.
Dóchas	Committal prison for female prisoners aged 17 years and over at North Circular Road, Dublin 7
Limerick	Committal prison for adult male and female, at Mulgrave Street, Limerick.
Cork	Committal prison for adult male prisoners, at Rathmore Road, Cork.
Castlerea	Committal prison for adult male prisoners, at Harristown, Castlerea, Co. Roscommon.
Cloverhill	Committal prison for remand adult male prisoners, at Cloverhill Road, Clondalkin, Dublin 22
Arbour Hill	Prison for adult male prisoners, at Arbour Hill, Dublin 7.
Midlands	Prison for adult male prisoners, at Dublin Road, Portlaoise, Co. Laois.
Portlaoise	Prison for adult male prisoners, including the detention of high security prisoners, at Dublin Road, Portlaoise, Co. Laois
Wheatfield	Prison for adult male prisoners, at Cloverhill Road, Clondalkin. Dublin

Shelton Abbey	An open centre for male prisoners aged 19 years and over, at Arklow, Co. Wicklow
St. Patricks Institution	An institution for male juveniles aged 16 to 21 years, at North Circular Road, Dublin 7 (Closing down)
Loughan House	An open centre for the detention of male prisoners aged 18 years and over, at Blacklion, Co. Cavan
Training Unit	A semi-open place of detention for male prisoners aged 18 years and over, at Glengarriff Parade, Dublin 7, for industrial training.

An Introduction to Criminal Law in Ireland

Probation Service and the Irish Criminal Justice System

The Role of the Probation Service within the Irish Criminal Justice System

The Probation Service is an agency of the Department of Justice and Equality. The Probation Service is sometimes involved in the Criminal Justice Process between the prosecution and trial phase, for example when a court requires a Probation Officer to hold a family conference. More often, the Probation Service become involved in the criminal justice process between the trial and sanction phases, often in cases where a trial court requires a pre-sanction assessment and report to assist in deciding on an appropriate sanction. In some cases, the court may be considering placing an offender on probation supervision or community service.

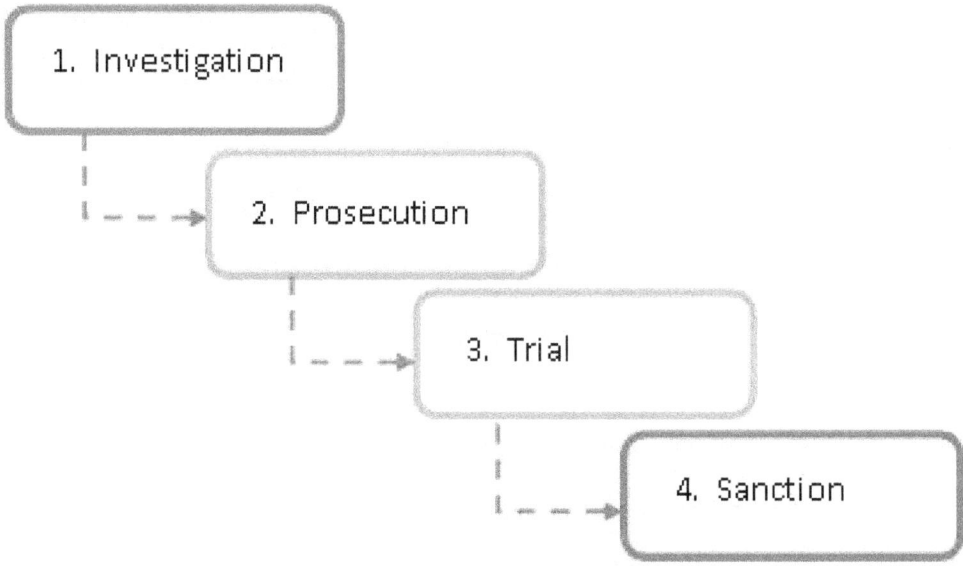

Where the court decides on a community-based sanction, The Probation Service is responsible for managing the sanction and supervising the offender. They help offenders to become better citizens and make good the harm done by crime. The Probation Service also undertakes whatever steps are appropriate to reduce the risk of future harm or re-offending by the offender.

The Probation Service has an important role in planning and preparing for the release of prisoners and their return to the community. They also supervise some offenders after their release from prison. This particular role is focused on reintegrating the offender in society, with the priority of protecting the public and reducing the risk of re-offending.

The Probation Service works closely with the other agencies of the criminal justice system, as illustrated in the diagram below, to reduce crime and make communities safer.

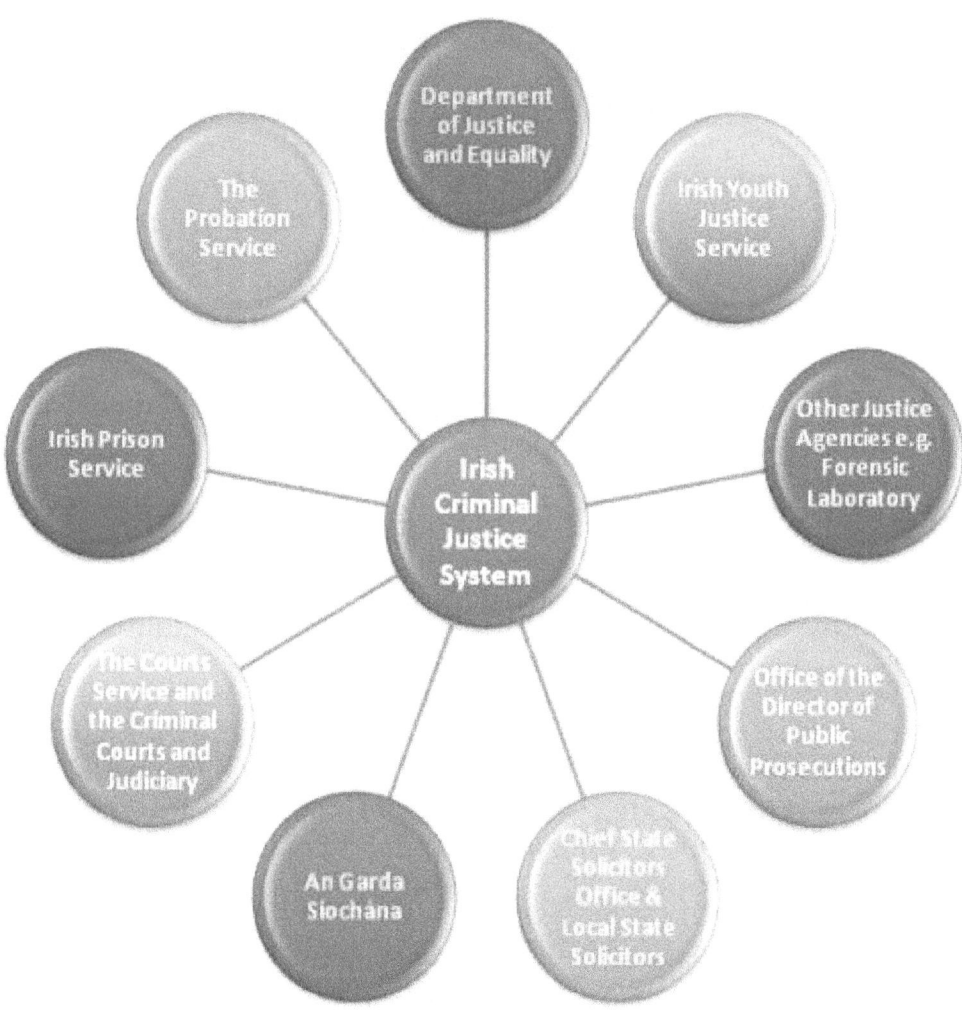

The Probation Service co-operates with criminal justice agencies in other jurisdictions, especially in cases where offenders move between countries.

Function of the Director of Public Prosecutions

The prosecution system in Ireland is not described or set out fully in any one document. It is grounded in the Constitution of Ireland, 1937 and in statute law, notably **the Prosecution of Offences Act, 1974**, which established the office of Director of Public Prosecutions. The prosecution system in Ireland has developed from common law tradition and many important practices and rules in Ireland have their basis in common law, that is, judge-made law.

Article 30.3 of the Constitution of Ireland provides as follows:

"All crimes and offences prosecuted in any court constituted under Article 34 of this Constitution other than a court of summary jurisdiction shall be prosecuted in the name of the People and at the suit of the Attorney General or some other person authorised in accordance with law to act for that purpose."

Section 9(2) of the Criminal Justice (Administration) Act, 1924 conferred on the Attorney General the power to conduct all prosecutions in any court of summary jurisdiction except those which were prosecuted by a Minister, Department of State or other person authorised by law.

The Prosecution of Offences Act, 1974 established the Director of Public Prosecutions as an officer authorised in accordance with law to act for the purpose of prosecuting in the name of the People as provided for in Article 30.3 of the Constitution. Section 3(1) of the 1974 Act provides as follows:

"Subject to the provisions of this Act, the Director shall perform all the functions capable of being performed in relation to criminal matters and in relation to election petitions and referendum petitions by the Attorney General immediately before the commencement of this section and references to the Attorney General in any statute or statutory instrument in force immediately before such commencement shall be construed accordingly."

The 1974 Act thereby conferred on the Director of Public Prosecutions the function of prosecuting both on indictment and summarily. All criminal prosecutions taken on indictment are taken in the name of the People and are prosecuted at the suit of the Director, except for a limited category of offences still prosecuted at the suit of the Attorney General.

Section 2(5) of the 1974 Act provides that the Director shall be independent in the performance of his functions. Section 6 of the Act underscores that independence by making it unlawful for persons other than defendants or complainants in criminal proceedings, or persons likely to be defendants, or their legal or medical advisers, members of their family or social workers, to communicate with the Director or his officers for the purpose of influencing the making of a decision to withdraw or not to initiate criminal proceedings or any particular charge in criminal proceedings.

The Director independently enforces the criminal law in the courts on behalf of the People of Ireland. To this end he directs and supervises public prosecutions on indictment in the courts and gives general direction and advice to the Garda Síochána in relation to summary cases and specific direction in such cases where requested. The Director decides whether to charge people with criminal offences, and what the charges should be. The Office of the Director of Public Prosecutions has defined its mission as "to provide on behalf of the People of Ireland a prosecution service that is independent, fair and effective".

The Office of the Director of Public Prosecutions consists of two legal divisions, the Directing Division and the Solicitors Division. There is also an Administration Division that provides the organisational, infrastructural, and administrative information services required by the Office. The Directing Division comprises a small number of professional officers, both barristers and solicitors, whose principal function is to make submissions to the Director and to take decisions in relation to the initiation or continuation of criminal prosecutions and to give on-going instructions and directions to the Solicitors Division, local State Solicitors and counsel regarding the conduct of criminal proceedings.

The work of appearing for the Director in court is carried out either by the full-time legal staff in the Solicitors Division who represent the Director in all courts in Dublin, or by the local State Solicitors in courts outside Dublin. The Solicitors Division is headed by the Chief Prosecution Solicitor who acts as solicitor to the Director. The Division consists of solicitors and legal executives whose responsibilities include:

- preparation of and conducting summary cases on behalf of the Director in all courts sitting in Dublin;
- implementation of directions from the Directing Division;
- preparation of books of evidence in indictable cases;

- briefing, assisting and instructing barristers nominated to conduct prosecutions;
- attending trials and reporting outcomes to the Directing Division;
- providing a liaison service to agencies and parties involved in the criminal process;
- consenting to certain cases being dealt with summarily rather than on indictment.

Criminal cases are divided into two types - indictable offences and summary offences.

Indictable offences:

- are the more serious cases;
- are heard by a judge and jury in the Circuit Criminal Court or the Central Criminal Court;
- carry the most serious penalties if the court convicts the suspect;
- can sometimes be dealt with in the Special Criminal Court by three judges sitting without a jury;
- are subject to appeal to the Court of Criminal Appeal.

Summary offences:

- are less serious offences;
- are heard by a judge without a jury in the District Court and on appeal in the Circuit Court;
- cannot be subject to a maximum prison sentence of more than 12 months for any one offence or 24 months for 2 or more offences.

The conduct of trials on indictment is handled by counsel practising at the bar,(*barristers*) who are engaged (*paid or contracted*) to represent (*be on the side of*) the Director on a case by case basis. Counsel prosecutes in accordance with the Director's instructions. (*the barrister prosecutes whoever the DPP decides "who they have a case against"*)

Most summary prosecutions brought in the District Court are brought in the name of the Director. In practice the great majority are presented by officers of the Garda Síochána without specific reference to the Director's Office except in cases where the Garda Síochána are required to seek a direction from the Director or where for some other reason they seek instructions. Under ***section***

8 of the Garda Síochána Act 2005, members of the Garda Síochána who prosecute summarily in the course of their official duties must do so in the name of the Director of Public Prosecutions and must comply with any directions given by the Director, whether of a general or specific nature. The Director may assume the conduct of a prosecution instituted by a Garda at any time.

Except for certain duties which arise under **the Garda Síochána (Complaints) Act, 1986** where an investigation is being carried out into an alleged offence by a member of the Garda Síochána, the Director of Public Prosecutions has no investigative function. In the Irish criminal justice system the investigation of criminal offences is the function of the Garda Síochána. In addition, there are specialised investigating authorities in relation to certain particular categories of crime, including the Competition Authority in relation to offences against the Competition Acts; the investigation branch of the Revenue Commissioners in relation to revenue offences; the Health and Safety Authority in relation to offences relating to safety and welfare at work; and the Office of Director of Corporate Enforcement which deals with offences against company law. This list is not exhaustive. Complaints of criminal conduct made to the Director cannot be investigated by him but are transmitted to the Garda Commissioner or to one of the other investigation authorities to take the appropriate decisions and action. While the Director has no investigative function, he and his Office cooperate regularly with the Garda Síochána and the other investigating agencies during the course of criminal investigations, particularly in furnishing relevant legal and procedural advice.

Many investigative agencies have the power to prosecute summarily without reference to the Director. The sole power to prosecute on indictment rests with the Director (apart from cases still dealt with by the Attorney General). When an offence is or may be sufficiently serious to be tried on indictment, the investigator sends a file to the Director. The decision whether to initiate or continue a criminal prosecution is made by the Director or one of his professional officers who decide independently of those who were responsible for the investigation what, if any, charges to bring. In some cases a summary prosecution may be directed.

An Introduction to Criminal Law in Ireland

The Prosecution of Crime

Most criminal prosecutions in Ireland are brought by the DPP (Director of Public Prosecutions) although other entities can also prosecute crime in Ireland.

The Attorney General, Dublin City Council, the Competition Authority and others also have the power to bring criminal proceedings.

Generally, criminal proceedings are started in the District Court (although more serious offences can be initiated in the Special Criminal Court) and are started in one of two ways - by way of District Court summons or the charge sheet procedure.

District Court Summons Procedure

A District Court summons is basically an order to appear before the District Court to answer a complaint.

This complaint will have been made by a member of An Garda Siochana and on foot of this complaint a District Court clerk will issue a summons for the attendance of the suspect before the District Court to answer the complaint.

The Validity of the Summons

In order for a summons to be valid it must

- State in ordinary language details of the offence of which the dependant is suspect
- It must give the offender the time, date and location of the District Court before which the dependant must appear.

Service of the summons can be carried out in person by a Garda or by post and it must be served 7 days before the Court date.

If there is a serious defect in the Summons, for example omitting the location of the court, then the summons will be struck out by the sitting Judge.

Time Limits for the Issuing of a Summons

The time limit for the issuing of a summons is that the complaint must be made to the District Court clerk within 6 months of the alleged offence, provided the offence is a minor or summary offence.

An Introduction to Criminal Law in Ireland

Indictable Offences Time Limits

Indictable offences do not have time limits imposed and can be prosecuted at any time after the alleged offence.

Charge Sheet Procedure

Offences can also be prosecuted by way of the charge sheet procedure in the District Court.

The charge sheet procedure involves the arrest of the alleged offender and transportation to the Garda station where the arrested person will be given a sheet which sets out the facts of the alleged offence and the charge.

Once the charge is read out to the suspect person, any remarks or comments made by him will be noted on the charge sheet.

The suspect person may be released on station bail, provided there are no outstanding warrants for his arrest.

If the suspect is released on bail he will have to enter a recognizance to compel his appearance before the next sitting of the District court. If he is refused bail he can apply for bail to the Judge at the District Court sitting before which he appears.

If the suspect person fails to appear a "bench warrant" will be issued by the Judge for the arrest of the suspect to bring him before the court to answer the charges against him.

Once the suspect is before the District Court the arresting Garda will give evidence of arrest, charge and caution and will also give evidence of any comments made by the suspect.

The charge sheet is then lodged with the District Court clerk.

- If the alleged offence is not a minor offence but an indictable offence the suspect may be sent to the Circuit Criminal Court, the Special Criminal Court or the Central Criminal Court.
- If the offender is in doubt as to whether they need a solicitor to represent them when facing a criminal charge, it can be stated that no matter what the charges the offender will need to have legal representation, it is critical to have legal representation in most circumstances.

Right to Silence and against Self-incrimination

The right to silence is closely connected to the presumption of innocence. The issue has been the subject of much debate and was considered by both the Committee reviewing *the Offences against the State Acts in 2002* and, more recently, by the Balance in the Criminal Law Review Group in 2007. In general terms a detained person is entitled to maintain silence on the basis that his or her silence will not be admissible in proceedings against him or her and a defendant cannot be compelled to give evidence in court, nor can the prosecution remark on this.

The right to silence in the face of questioning by a member of An Garda Síochána is not absolute. The law permits inferences adverse to the suspect to be drawn in proceedings from the suspect's failure to mention a defence on which he or she subsequently seeks to rely or from his or her failure or refusal to account for suspicious circumstances which clearly call for an answer. The law governing the drawing of inferences was amended in 2007[3] in order to expand its application to all arrestable offences (i.e., offences carrying a maximum sentence of imprisonment of 5 years or more) and to strengthen the system of safeguards.

This system of safeguards means that:

- only such inferences as are considered proper by the court may be drawn;
- the person cannot be convicted solely or mainly on such inferences;
- inferences may be treated only as corroboration, not as primary evidence;

The person must be warned in ordinary language that the question of an inference may arise and the person must have been afforded a reasonable opportunity to consult a solicitor before they decide to refuse to account; the interview must be recorded.

The Criminal Justice Bill 2011 contains proposals to strengthen the system of safeguards that applies by providing that the person must have been informed of his or her right to consult a solicitor and (*other than where he or she waived that right*) been afforded an opportunity to do so.

Bail

Bail is based on the principle that the suspect is presumed innocent until proven guilty. Where a suspect person has been detained in custody prior to the first court appearance, the prosecutor, in addition to considering the charges to be presented to the court, is required to consider any continuing need to remand that person in custody. **The Bail Act 1997** provides: *'when an application for bail is made by a person charged with a serious offence, the court may refuse the application if the court is satisfied that such refusal is reasonably considered necessary to prevent the commission of a serious offence by that person.'* Bail can also be refused where there is a danger that the suspect might abscond or interfere with witnesses. If there is a serious breach of a condition attached to the granting of bail, the prosecutor may seek its revocation.

Arrest Defined

> *An arrest is the act of depriving a person of his or her liberty usually in relation to the purported investigation and prevention of crime, also defined as keeping of a person in custody by legal authority.*

Arrests

An arrest is the apprehending or restraining of a person to bring that person to a District Court within a reasonable time

The offender cannot be arrested for the purpose of gathering evidence or 'helping the Gardaí with their enquiries'.

The offender must be told why they are being arrested, for example, because the offender is suspected of having stolen goods. However, if the offender is arrested under **Section 30 of the Offences Against the State Act 1939**, they do not have to be told exactly why they are being arrested, the offender need only be told that they are being arrested under that section.

If the offender goes voluntarily to a Garda station, to assist the Gardaí with their enquiries, and are subjected to questioning or interrogation, the offender must be told and it must be clear to them that they are free to leave the station at any time unless they are arrested.

Often an arrest is on foot of a warrant. However, a warrant is not always necessary.

Arrest without a warrant

The offender may be arrested without a warrant when a Garda, with reasonable cause, suspects that an arrestable offence has been committed and that the offender is guilty of the offence. An 'arrestable offence' is an offence for which the penalty, for a person who has no previous convictions, can be 5 years imprisonment or more. Specific laws give the Gardaí powers of arrest as well. For example, a Garda can arrest the offender under the Road Traffic Acts without a warrant if he/she suspects that the offender is committing an offence in relation to drinking and driving.

Entry and search of premises, to carry out an arrest

If a Garda has obtained a warrant to arrest the offender, he or she may enter and search any premises where he or she suspects the offender to be. He or she must identify himself or herself, demand entry and state why he or she is there. If the Garda is refused entry, he or she may break open outer and inner doors to get in.

When a Garda does not have an arrest warrant, he or she may enter and search any premises where he or she, with reasonable cause, suspects the offender to be. However, if the premises are a dwelling, and he or she does not have the permission of the person who lives in the dwelling, the Garda cannot enter unless:

- The offender lives at the dwelling
- The Garda has seen the offender inside or entering the dwelling or
- The Garda, with reasonable cause, suspects that before he or she can get an arrest warrant, the offender will either abscond or the offender will obstruct the course of justice or
- He or she, with reasonable cause, suspects that before he or she can get an arrest warrant, the offender will commit an offence.

Manner of Arrest

Force can only be used to make an arrest if it is absolutely necessary.

When a Garda arrests the offender, he or she will actually touch the offender's body or otherwise restrain the offender's liberty. If the offender is arrested on a criminal charge, the offender must be informed at the time the offender is arrested of the charge unless this is very clear (*for example, if the offender is arrested while committing an offence*).

After the offender have been charged, the Garda must caution them with the following words: "You are not obliged to say anything unless you wish to do so, but whatever you say will be taken down in writing and may be given in evidence."

When the offender is brought to the Garda station, details of the offence must be set out in a 'charge sheet'. A copy of the details must be given to the offender. The Garda will formally charge the offender by reading each charge over to them, and they will be cautioned after each charge is read out. The Garda must keep a note of any reply the offender makes.

Search of the Arrested Person

A Garda may search the offender after the arrest and take:

- articles that he or she believes to be connected with, or evidence relating to, the offence charged or
- articles that he or she believes to be connected with, or evidence relating to, some other offence or
- articles that the offender might use to injure another person or property or to escape

Procedure after Arrest

Once the offender are charged and cautioned, they must be released on bail by the member in charge of the station (a form of bail known as station bail) and transferred from the Garda Station to the District Court as soon as reasonably possible. If the offender is arrested after 5 p.m. they may be brought to the District Court as early as possible before noon the following day. At the District Court, the offender may be released on bail or remanded in custody by the judge.

Only in certain specific circumstances may the offender be detained in a Garda Station for a length of time before being brought to court. Under the *Criminal Justice Act 1984*, the offender may be detained in a Garda Station for up to 12 hours. The offence of which the offender is suspected must be one that may be punishable by imprisonment for at least 5 years. The 12-hour period runs from the time of the offender arrest but the offender may agree to a rest period between 12 midnight and 8 am and this will not be included in the 12 hours.

In general, if the offender is arrested they do not have to say anything. However, if the offender is detained under **the Criminal Justice Act 1984** they must tell the Gardaí their name and address.

The Gardaí have no general power to take fingerprints or take forensic tests. They may do these things if the offender consent or if they have specific power under specific laws, for example, under **the Offences Against the State Act** or **the Criminal Law (Jurisdiction) Act of 1976**. Under Section 30 of the Offences Against the State Act the offender may be detained for up to 48 hours before being brought to Court. If the offender is detained, they must be informed of their right to consult a solicitor.

Immunity from Arrest

Ambassadors and their suites and other diplomatic agents who represent foreign governments while living in this country cannot be arrested.

Members of each House of the Oireachtas cannot be arrested while going to, returning from or within the confines of either House of the Oireachtas, except in the case of treason, felony or breach of peace.

An arrestable offence under the Criminal Law Act 1997

In Ireland, **the Criminal Law Act 1997** abolished the terms felony and misdemeanour and created the term *"arrestable offence"* in their place.

Section 2 of the Criminal Law Act, 1997 defines an arrestable offence as follows:

"arrestable offence" means an offence for which a person of full capacity and not previously convicted may, under or by virtue of any enactment, be punished by imprisonment for a term of five years or by a more severe penalty and includes an attempt to commit any such offence

Section 30 of the Offences Against The State Act 1939

Under **Section 30 of the Offences against the State Act 1939** (as amended), a Garda may arrest a suspect (who it is suspected has committed one or more of certain offences) and take him/her to a Garda Station for questioning.

Periods of Detention:

72 Hours - Maximum Period of Detention

24 Hours – Granted by Arresting Member

24 Hours – Extended by Chief Superintendent

24 Hours – Application by Superintendent at the District Court

This can happen and, usually involves firearms or explosives offences. Normally used for murder enquiries, and the investigation of terrorist / subversive offences.

Section 30 of the Offences against the State Act 1939

If the offender are arrested under s.30 of the Offences Against the State Act 1939

Initial period = 24 hours + 24 hours extension (authorised by Chief Superintendent)

2 days detention on Garda authority + 24 hours extension (authorised by District Court judge)

Total = 3 days (72 hours)

Section 4 of the Criminal Justice Act 1984

4.—(1) This section applies to any offence for which a person of full age and capacity and not previously convicted may, under or by virtue of any enactment, be punished by imprisonment for a term of five years or by a more severe penalty and to an attempt to commit any such offence.

2. Where a member of the Garda Síochána arrests without warrant a person whom he, with reasonable cause, suspects of having committed an offence to which this section applies, that person may be taken to, and detained in, a Garda Síochána station for such period as is authorised by this section if the member of the Garda Síochána in charge of the station to which he is taken on arrest has, at the time of that person's arrival at the station, reasonable grounds for believing that his detention is necessary for the proper investigation of the offence.

3 (a) The period for which a person so arrested may be detained shall, subject to the provisions of this section, not exceed six hours from the time of his arrest.

    a) An officer of the Garda Síochána not below the rank of superintendent may direct that a person detained pursuant to subsection (2) be detained for a further period not exceeding six hours if he has reasonable grounds for believing that such further detention is necessary for the proper investigation of the offence.

    b) A direction under paragraph (b) may be given orally or in writing and if given orally shall be recorded in writing as soon as practicable.

(4) If at any time during the detention of a person pursuant to this section there are no longer reasonable grounds for suspecting that he has committed an offence to which this section applies, he shall be released from custody forthwith unless his detention is authorised apart from this Act.

(5) Where a member of the Garda Síochána has enough evidence to prefer a charge with an offence against a person detained in a Garda Síochána station pursuant to this section, he shall without delay charge that person or cause him to be charged unless that person is, with reasonable cause, suspected of another offence to which this section applies and the member of the Garda Síochána then in charge of the station has reasonable grounds for believing that the continuance of his detention pursuant to this section is necessary for the proper investigation of that offence.

(6) (a) If a person is being detained pursuant to this section in a Garda Síochána station between midnight and 8 a.m. and the member in charge of the station is of the opinion that any questioning of that person for the purpose of the investigation should be suspended in order to afford him reasonable time to rest, and that person consents in writing to such suspension, the member may give him a notice in writing (which shall specify the time at which it is given) that the investigation (so far as it involves questioning of him) is suspended until such time as is specified in the notice and shall ask him to sign the notice as an acknowledgement that he has received it; and, if the notice is given, the period between the giving thereof and the time specified therein (not being a time later than 8 a.m.) shall be excluded in reckoning a period of detention permitted by this section and the powers conferred by section 6 shall not be exercised during the period so excluded: "Provided that not more than one notice under this paragraph shall be given to a person during any period between midnight and 8 a.m."

    b) A notice under paragraph (a) may, for serious reasons, be withdrawn by a subsequent notice given in like manner, and in that event any time subsequent to the giving of the second notice shall not be excluded under that paragraph.

c) A member of the Garda Síochána when giving a notice to any person under paragraph (a) or (b) shall explain to him orally the effect of the notice.

d) The following particulars shall be entered in the records of the Garda Síochána station without delay—

i. the time of the giving of a notice under paragraph (a) and the time specified therein as the time up to which the questioning is being suspended,

ii. whether the person being detained acknowledged that he received the notice, and

iii. the time of the giving of any notice under paragraph (b).

e) Records kept in pursuance of paragraph (d) shall be preserved for at least twelve months and, if any proceedings are taken against the person in question for the offence in respect of which he was detained, until the conclusion of the proceedings (including any appeal or retrial).

(7) (a) Subject to paragraph (b), subsection (2) shall not apply to a person below the age of twelve years.

b) If the member in charge of the Garda Síochána station in which a person is detained has reasonable grounds for believing that the person is not below the age of twelve years the subsection shall apply to him as if he were of that age, provided that, where such member ascertains or has reasonable grounds for believing that the person is below that age, he shall be released from custody forthwith unless his detention is authorised apart from this Act.

(8) Where it appears to a member of the Garda Síochána that a person arrested in the circumstances mentioned in subsection (2) is in need of medical attention, or where during his detention it comes to notice that he is in need of such attention, and he is taken for that purpose to a hospital or other suitable place, the time before his arrival at the station or the time during which he is absent from the station, as the case may be, shall be excluded in reckoning a period of detention permitted by this section.

(9) To avoid doubt, it is hereby declared that a person who is being detained pursuant to subsection (2) in connection with an offence shall in no case be held in detention (whether for the investigation of that or any other offence) for longer than twelve hours from the time of his arrest, not including any period which is to be excluded under subsection (6) or (8) in reckoning a period of detention.

(10) Nothing in this section shall affect the operation of *section 30 of the Act of 1939*.

(11) The powers conferred by this section are without prejudice to any powers exercisable by a member of the Garda Síochána in relation to offences other than offences to which this section applies.

6

---

[6] Irish Statute Book

Section 2 - Drug Trafficking Act 1996

Drug offences

The primary legislation under which criminal charges for drugs offences is brought is *the Misuse of Drugs Act 1977* and the *Misuse of Drugs Act, 1984*. These have been further amended by *the Criminal Justice Act 1999*, *the Criminal Justice Act 2006* and *the Criminal Justice Act 2007*. *The Misuse of Drugs Regulations 1988 (SI 328 of 1988)* (as amended) lists the various substances to which the legislation applies. *The Criminal Justice (Psychoactive Substances) Act 2010* covers substances which are not specifically proscribed under the Misuse of Drugs Acts, but which have psychoactive effects.

The main drug offences under which criminal charges are brought are offences of drug possession and possession for the purpose of supply.

Role of the Garda Siochana in combating drug abuse and drug trafficking

The work of the Criminal Assets Bureau, established in 1996, has been very successful in seizing the assets of those convicted of drug trafficking. The Garda Siochana has also established the National Drugs Unit to target national and international drugs trafficking. At local level, Local Drugs Units police the drugs situation and Garda juvenile liaison officers work with the offending people to try and prevent them getting involved with drugs. In some Local Drugs Task Force areas, Community Policing Forces have been set up to deal with the drug problem with the help of the community. In October 2008 Dial to Stop Drug Dealing was launched. This initiative tackled drug dealing in local communities by providing a confidential and completely anonymous way for someone to pass on information on drug dealing in their local community to the Gardaí.

The National Crime Council advises on policy matters of drug-related crime and drug prevention. The Gardaí are also involved in a number of awareness-raising programmes such as the Garda Schools Programme, the Garda Mobile Anti-Drugs Unit and the Juvenile Diversion Programme.

Role of the Customs and Excise service in combating drug trafficking

The Customs and Excise services are responsible for detecting and seizing controlled drugs at importation. There is close co-operation between the Gardaí and the Custom and Excise services in the area of drug law enforcement and a joint task force involving the Gardaí, the Customs and Excise Services and the Naval Services has been set up. These bodies liaise at a local level to prevent drug trafficking. The Customs and Excise services are involved in the Multi-Disciplinary Group on Organised Crime and are also very involved in the operation of the Criminal Assets Bureau with the Gardaí. The Customs National Drug Team was set up by the Revenue Commissioners in 1992 to tackle the illegal importation of drugs into Ireland.

Customs National Drug Team

The Customs National Drug Team (CNDT) concentrates solely on combating the importation of illegal drugs into Ireland. The CNDT has its Head Office located in Dublin and intelligence units, operational units, maritime units and drug detector dog units that are strategically placed at all major ports and airports and at various coastal locations nation-wide. All CNDT units are mobile and can be deployed to other locations as necessary. The CNDT is supported by outfield officials who are also responsible for the detection and prevention of drug smuggling as part of their normal duties.

Possession of controlled drugs - cannabis or cannabis resin

Under the Misuse of Drugs Acts anyone found in possession of cannabis or cannabis resin is guilty of an offence. If the court decides that the drug was for personal use and not for sale or distribution and this was a first offence, it can impose a class D fine on summary conviction in a District Court. On conviction on indictment, the defendant can be fined €1,270. For a second offence, a class D fine may be imposed and on conviction on indictment, a fine of €2,540 can be imposed. For a third or subsequent conviction, a class C fine can be imposed. If the court decides, a prison sentence of not more than 12 months can be imposed as well. On conviction on indictment, the court may decide on an appropriate fine and/or a prison sentence of up to three years can be imposed.

Possession of any other controlled drugs

It is an offence to be in possession of a controlled drug and on summary conviction for this offence; the offender could be liable for a class C fine or a prison sentence of no longer than 12 months. If the court decides, the offender could be liable for both. On conviction on indictment for possessing controlled drugs, the court can decide on an appropriate fine and the offender could also be liable for a prison sentence of not more than seven years. Again, if the court decides, the offender could be liable for both.

Growing cannabis plants or opium poppies

It is also an offence to grow cannabis plants or opium poppies and on summary conviction for this offence, the offender could be liable for a class C fine or a prison sentence of no longer than 12 months. If the court decides, the offender could be liable for both. On conviction on indictment for growing these plants, the court can decide on an appropriate fine and the offender could also be liable for a prison sentence of not more than 14 years. Again, if the court decides, the offender could be liable for both.

Regulations regarding opium

It is an offence to use prepared opium (e.g., heroin) for illegal use, to go to a place for the purposes of using opium or to have any paraphernalia (pipes, utensils) associated with illegal opium use in the offender possession. On summary conviction for this offence, the offender could be liable for a class C fine or a prison sentence of no longer than 12 months. If the court decides, the offender could be liable for both. On conviction on indictment for this offence, the court can decide on an appropriate fine and the offender could also be liable for a prison sentence of no more than 14 years. Again, if the court decides, the offender could be liable for both.

Possession of controlled drugs for sale or supply

Under the legislation, it is an offence to be in possession of a controlled drug with the intention of selling it illegally. Anyone found guilty of this offence is liable to a class C fine on summary conviction in a District Court. If the court decides, he or she could be subject to a fine and a prison term not exceeding 12 months. On conviction on indictment for this offence, the court can decide on an appropriate fine. The court can also impose a life sentence for this offence if it decides it is necessary. However, lesser sentences can also be imposed, either with a fine or without.

Where the market value of the drugs is €13,000 or more, the person convicted is liable for a minimum sentence of 10 years. This does not apply, however, where the court is satisfied there are exceptional circumstances. Similar penalties apply to someone convicted of importing drugs with a value of €13,000 or more.

Anyone found guilty of supplying or attempting to supply a controlled drug into a prison, children detention school or remand centre can receive a class B fine on summary conviction or a prison term not exceeding 12 months, or both. On conviction on indictment, the court can impose an appropriate fine or a maximum prison term of 10 years, or both.

Under *the Criminal Justice (Psychoactive Substances) Act 2010* it is an offence to sell or supply for human consumption substances which are not specifically proscribed under *the Misuse of Drugs Acts*, but which have psychoactive effects. Anyone found guilty of such an offence is liable for a class A fine on summary conviction or a prison for a term not exceeding 12 months or both. On conviction on indictment they can be fined or imprisoned for a term not exceeding 5 years or both.

Use of premises, vehicles or vessels for certain activities

Anyone who occupies or controls any land, vehicle or vessel and is found guilty of allowing it to be used for activities such as the manufacture, importation or supply of a controlled drug is liable on summary conviction to a class C fine or a prison sentence of no longer than 12 months or both. On conviction on indictment for this offence, the court can impose an appropriate fine or a prison sentence of no more than 14 years or both.

Forged or fraudulently altered prescriptions

It is an offence to forge a prescription or to try to change it in any way in order to deceive. Anyone found guilty of this offence is liable, on summary conviction, to a class D fine or a prison sentence not exceeding six months. If the court decides, the offender could be liable for both. On conviction on indictment for this offence, the court can decide on an appropriate fine and/or impose a prison term not exceeding three years.

Attempting or helping others to commit an offence

It is an offence to attempt to commit a drug offence covered by the legislation, or to help or incite someone else to commit the drug offence. If the offender are found guilty the offender are liable to be sentenced as if the offender had committed the drug offence.

Court-ordered drug treatment

For some drugs offences, (illegal possession of controlled drugs, possession of controlled drugs for unlawful sale or supply, breaking the regulations regarding opium, growing opium poppies or cannabis plants or forging or fraudulently altering prescriptions), the court may decide that imposing the usual penalties is not the most effective response. The court can remand the offender for whatever period it considers necessary (no longer than eight days if they are being held in custody). During this time, the court can ask the Health Service Executive (HSE), a Probation officer or other qualified person to prepare a medical report and/or a report on the offenders vocational, educational and social circumstances. They may also be asked to make recommendations for the offender treatment.

Based on the findings of these reports, the court may decide not to impose a fine or prison sentence on the offender. Instead, the offender may be placed under the supervision of a named person or body (such as the HSE) for a specified period of time, or they may be required to get the kind of treatment (medical or otherwise) that has been recommended for them. The court may also order that they complete a course of education, instruction or training that will improve their job prospects or social circumstances, facilitate their social rehabilitation or reduce the likelihood of them committing further drugs offences.

Depending on the circumstances of their case, the court may order that they be detained in a specialised custodial treatment centre. The period the offender can be held for depends on the offence. The offender cannot be held for longer than a year, but if the maximum period of imprisonment that the court may impose for a particular crime is shorter than a year, the offender can only be held for that period of time.

If the court decides it is in the offender best interests, they may not be allowed to see the contents of any report that has been prepared on their case. However, the report will be made available to the offender barrister or solicitor.

If the offender ignores an order of the court, they can be detained in a custodial treatment centre or have the usual penalties for their offence (fines and/or imprisonment) imposed on them.

If the offender have been sent to a custodial treatment centre by a court order, they can make an application to the court that detention is no longer in their best interests or in the best interests of other people at the centre. Based on this application, the court can review the offender case and revoke the detention order. The court then has a number of options open to it. If the court decides that the offender are still in need of treatment, it can order the offender continued detention, possibly in another treatment centre. If custodial treatment is not considered necessary, the offender may be ordered to continue treatment but not on a custodial basis.

The court can also decide to impose the usual penalties (prison sentence and/or fine) under the Misuse of Drugs Act for the offence if it considers it appropriate to do so. This will depend on the circumstances of the offender case and if a prison sentence is imposed, the court must take into account the amount of time the offender have already been detained in a treatment centre. The court also has the option of not imposing any penalty if it is satisfied that the offender is no longer in need of treatment and that the circumstances of the case do not warrant further penalties.

Chapter 3

Homicide

The Definition of Homicide

Homicide, in law, is any killing of one person by another. The word is from the Latin, and means "man-killing." Homicide is a legal term that describes murder, manslaughter or any unlawful killing.

Murder involves the situation where a person kills another person unlawfully and where the mental element - as defined in **the Criminal Justice Act 1964** - was that they *"intended to kill, or cause serious injury to, some person, whether the person was actually killed or not."*

Manslaughter is any other unlawful killing and is currently defined – at common law – by reference to two categories, voluntary and involuntary manslaughter.

Murder = Actus Reus + Mens Rea

Manslaughter = Actus Reus

Mens Rea means the guilty mind or wrongful intention and, is ***discovered in the definition of the offence; it is words like 'intention', 'recklessly', 'with malice aforethought'.***

When interpreting statutes, it is a Common Law presumption that Mens Rea is necessary in all crimes.

Actus Reus is the conduct of the suspect. It can be an act of commission or act of omission, and it must be a voluntary act that causes the damage or harm. It can also be a "state of affairs".

A person may incur criminal liability for failing to do that which the law requires him to do as much as by doing that which the law prohibits.

Actus Reus includes the state of affairs or circumstances surrounding the commission of the offence, together with the results or consequences (if any) that flows from that act or omission. It is essential that the defendant acted voluntarily and that he caused the injury, damage or harm.

In other words, Actus Reus includes all the elements of the offence indicated in the definition except the Mens Rea (the state of mind), if any.

- Must be a voluntary act, not automatism

Generally the suspect's conduct must be a voluntary act or omission, and he will not be held liable for acts done in a state of automatism. Automatism resulting from self-induced intoxication is no excuse.

- The suspect must cause the prohibited consequences.
- The crime must be caused by some conduct by the suspect.
- That conduct need not be a direct cause of the crime, but can be through the agency of others.
- The conduct needs not be the sole or the effective cause of the crime, provided it cannot be dismissed as trivial, or as merely events leading up to the commission of the crime.
- An omission is only culpable if there is a common law or statutory duty to act.

- Generally, there is no obligation on anyone to prevent harm or wrongdoing.
- Omissions are only criminal where a duty to act arises at common law or is imposed by statute.

What is Murder?

Murder refers to the unlawful killing of another human being with intent or a purpose or "**malice aforethought** (*a conscious intent to cause death or great bodily harm to another person*)". Usually, this state of mind differentiates murder from other kinds of unlawful homicide, for example manslaughter. For there to be a conviction of Murder there has to be the element of Intent.

What is Manslaughter?

It is the unlawful killing of human being where the intention which is necessary for murder is absent; it may be (a) voluntary or (b) involuntary.

Voluntary Manslaughter:

This happens when two people get into a sudden fight, and one had the upper hand, say one had a baseball bat. Who started the fight is irrelevant; the fatal blow is the important issue.

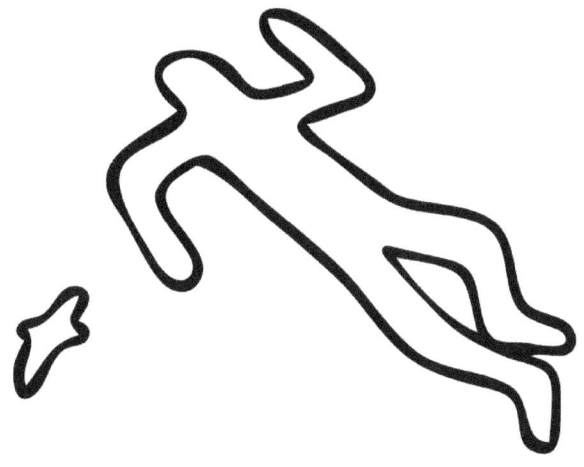

"If a man entered into a fight with an unarmed man, intending to avail himself of a deadly weapon and in the use of such weapon kills his opponent, it is murder; but if he had no such intention, and used the weapon in the heat of passion as a consequence of the attack made on him it is manslaughter. Whereas if he used it in defence of his own life and its use was as such necessary in the circumstances, he having no means of escape and no other means of resistance, then it is excusable homicide". See the People *(D.P.P.) -v- McEoin*

Voluntary manslaughter currently comprises a number of sub-categories. First, where all the elements of murder are established but the jury is satisfied that the suspect acted under provocation when he or she killed the other person.

Second, where all the elements of murder are established but the jury is satisfied that excessive force was used by the suspect in self-defence.

D.P.P.-v- Wayne O' Donoghue, [2006] IECCA 134 (2006). The respondent was tried and convicted on a charge of murder of the victim contrary to common law and to ***s.4 of the Criminal Justice Act 1964***. He was acquitted of murder but convicted of manslaughter as the Court affirmed that the respondent had no intention or "Mens Rea" "guilty mind" to kill.

Third, where - pursuant to **the Criminal Law (Insanity) Act 2006,** - a plea of diminished responsibility is established in answer to a charge of murder or infanticide. Involuntary manslaughter currently comprises two sub-categories. First, manslaughter by an unlawful and dangerous act, where the killing involves an act constituting a criminal offence, carrying with it the risk of bodily harm to the person killed. Involuntary Manslaughter occurs where a person by acting unlawfully, but with no intention of even hurting anyone, causes the death of another. It may arise;

(1) in doing an unlawful act e.g. killing a person by recklessly driving a motor car; or

(2) omission to discharge a legal duty, e.g., where a railway points man falls asleep and forgets to move the points and as a result a railway passenger is killed; or

(3) doing a lawful act negligently, as where a person indulges in rifle practice in the immediate vicinity of houses, or a parent causes his child's death by unreasonably chastising him with a reasonable instrument.

The second sub-category is manslaughter by gross negligence, where the killing arose from a negligent act or omission by the suspect involving a high risk of substantial personal injury.

Section 4 of the Criminal Justice Act, 1964, which provides:

4. (1) Where a person kills another unlawfully the killing shall not be murder unless the suspect person intended to kill, or cause serious injury to, some person, whether the person was actually killed or not.

(2)   The suspect person shall be presumed to have intended the natural and probable consequences of his conduct; but this presumption may be rebutted.

Section 4 of the Criminal Justice Act, 1964, defines the mental element in murder as "an intention to kill or cause serious injury". There is, apparently, little Irish authority on intention, but, in England, intention has been interpreted as embracing, in addition to situations where it is the actor's conscious object or purpose to kill, situations where, although it may not be the actor's object or purpose to kill, he nevertheless foresees death as virtually certain to result from his actions.

It is unclear what exactly "intention" means in Irish law, and the Law Reform Commission report states that, because of the scarcity of reported Irish authority on the matter, it is difficult to give a precise answer to the question as to what intention means.

The Irish courts have a strong tendency to require knowledge (or - at the very least - that the defendant "consciously disregarded a substantial and unjustifiable risk") in respect of each aspect of the actus reus of an offence **(see People (DPP) v Murray [1977] IR 360 (SC) 404.** *Henchy J.)The only exception (to what) would appear to be where the legislative history of the offence shows a clear intention to dispense with some part of the requirement of mens rea (as in* **CC v Ireland [2006] 4 IR 1 (SC)** which may, as in that case, lead to the provision being found to be unconstitutional.

A life sentence is mandatory for murder

Capital Punishment

Capital punishment was partially abolished in Ireland in 1964, for all but a few very specific forms of murder, notably the murder of Garda or prison officers. The Dáil finally abolished it completely in 1990, when new legislation created a 40-year minimum prison term for exceptional murders. The charge was then of Statutory or Common Murder.

People v Murray [1977] IR 360. Husband and wife Noel and Marie Murray were convicted of the Capital Murder of Garda Michael Reynolds in St Anne's Park, Dublin in 1975. Seeing as it was Capital murder both were sentenced to die by the non-jury Special Criminal Court.

"A provisional date was set for their execution, and they spent several months in the uncertainty of the death-cell before their appeal resulted in a substitution of a sentence of life imprisonment. The appeal court ruled that as the Murray couple, who had been involved in a bank robbery, were not aware at the time that Guard Reynolds — who had tried to apprehend them while off duty and in plain clothes — was in fact a Garda, the question of capital murder could not arise. Thus, the death sentence was set aside in this case.

Death Penalty Facts

- *The death penalty was abolished in law in the Republic of Ireland in 1990.*
- The Twenty-First Amendment of the Constitution Act, 2001, prohibited the death penalty and provided for the removal of references to the death penalty in the constitution.
- During the Civil War, 1921-23, the Free State government ordered the execution of 81 Anti-Treaty Republicans.
- Extra-judicial executions were also common at this time.
- Between the end of the Civil War in 1923 and the last execution in 1954 there were 35 executions in the State.
- Between 1939 and 1945 there were six executions under emergency legislation.
- Two of these executions were for a non-murder crime.
- The last man to be hanged in the State was Michael Manning.
  He was hanged at Mountjoy Prison, Dublin on 20 April, 1954.
  The hangman was Albert Pierrepoint.
- The last woman to be hanged in the State was Annie Walsh.
  She was hanged at Mountjoy Prison, Dublin in August, 1925.

She was the only woman hanged between independence in 1923 and the abolition of the death penalty in 1990.

- The last burning at the stake in Ireland was in 1353.
- The last beheading was Robert Emmet who was hanged and then beheaded.
- The last public hanging was in 1866.
- The last people to be sentenced to death in the State were INLA members Noel Callan and Michael McHugh for the capital murder of Garda Sergeant Patrick Morrissey on 27 June, 1985.
- The death sentence in their case was commuted to 40 years in prison without remission.
- On 15 April, 2011 Noel Callan lost his High Court appeal to be considered for remission. Mr Justice Michael Hanna ruled that he must serve the full 40 years.

Manslaughter and Provocation

A Murder charge, under certain circumstances, can be reduced to manslaughter. For example if adequate provocation is established, a murder charge may be reduced to manslaughter. Generally, there are four conditions that must be fulfilled to warrant the reduction: (1) the provocation must cause rage or fear in a reasonable person; (2) the defendant must have been provoked; (3) there should not be a time period between the provocation and the killing within which a reasonable person would cool off; and (4) the defendant should not have cooled off during that period.

Provocation is justifiable if ***a reasonable person under similar circumstances would be induced to act in the same manner as the defendant***. It must be found that the degree of ***provocation was such that a reasonable person would lose self-control***. In actual fact, there is no precise formula for determining reasonableness. It is a matter that is determined by the courts, either the jury, or the judge in a nonjury trial, after a full consideration of the evidence.

Certain forms of provocation that frequently arise have traditionally been considered reasonable or unreasonable by the courts.

A killing that results from anger that is induced by a violent blow with a fist or weapon might constitute sufficient provocation, provided the suspect did not incite the victim. It is not reasonable, however, to respond similarly to a light blow. A killing that results from mutual combat is often considered manslaughter, provided it was caused by the heat of passion aroused by the combat. An illegal arrest of one who knows of or believes in his or her innocence may provoke a reasonable person,

Although some cases are in dispute, on the issue of whether such an arrest would justify a killing. An attempt to make a legal arrest in an unlawful manner by the use of unnecessary violence might also constitute a heat of passion killing that will mitigate an intentional killing. Some cases have held that a reasonable belief that one's spouse is committing ADULTERY will suffice. An injury to persons in a close relationship to the suspect, such as a spouse, child, or parent, is often held to constitute reasonable provocation, particularly when the injury occurs in the suspect person's presence.

Fatal Assault Manslaughter

Fatal Assault Manslaughter occurs when a person is assaulted by another which was not pre meditated and the victim dies.

If there was intention, it is murder, but if he had no such intention, and used the weapon in the heat of the moment as a consequence of the attack made on him, it is manslaughter.

Case reference: *A Dublin man who pleaded guilty to the manslaughter of a man in an unprovoked attack near Dublin Airport has been jailed for 11 years. Ian Daly, 28, of Moatview Drive in Priorswood, had been on trial for the murder of Valerie Ranert. However, the Director of Public Prosecutions today accepted a plea of guilty to manslaughter. The Court heard how Mr Ranert and his girlfriend were in a car parked at a lay-by at Naul Road just north of Dublin Airport when a group of the offenders confronted them. The windows of Mr Ranert's car were kicked in. He was attacked in his car before being dragged outside and kicked about the head as he lay on the ground. Daly left his mobile phone at the scene and later fled to Spain after obtaining a false passport. He later returned and presented himself to Gardaí.*

Sentencing Daly this afternoon, Mr Justice George Birmingham said that the crime was one of 'gratuitous violence on a man who had been minding his own business.' He said Daly had embarked on 'intentional serious criminality', and that the crime was 'right at the upper end of the sentencing scale for manslaughter.' The court heard that in a written statement to detectives, Daly said he had given Mr Ranert two thumps and one kick. He said he could not remember who else was with him that night.

Criminal Negligence

This is described as, the failure to use reasonable care, to avoid consequences that threaten or harm the safety of the public, and that are the foreseeable outcome of acting in a particular manner. To be criminally negligent the suspect must have had the foresight to see the risk which is responsible for the illegal outcome.

Duty to Act

"If I see a man who is under my charge taking up a tumbler of poison, I should not become guilty of any crime by not stopping him. I am under no legal obligation to protect a stranger." **R v Paine**

As a general rule, we are not obliged to act, for anyone else's better or good, we are not even obliged to save a life unless we want to, however, I we attempt to help, we must follow through (if you start CPR, you must keep at it until the ambulance arrived),

Example*: If I was walking across O'Connell Bridge in Dublin, and should see a person in difficulty and believe they are drowning, I am under no obligation to help them unless I wish to do so, if I were to keep on walking there is no punishment in law for me...!!*

... the law only imposes liability for positive acts, however where a duty to act can be established it can then be proven that an omission constitutes an offence, criminal liability can occur. A person can be found guilty of a crime only if they possessed the essential Mens Rea and Actus Reus for committing the crime. Actus Reus is the "guilty deed or act" whereas Mens Rea is the associated "guilty mind".

A duty to Act (otherwise known as a duty not to commit an omission) creates an offence in criminal law.

Act or Omission

Firstly we need to identify if we are dealing with an act or an omission, was it a continuing act? If so these are acts and outside these notes, self-interest and personal autonomy must be outweighed by the law. It must also be noted that a person who is aware or ought to have been aware that he or she has created a dangerous situation and does nothing to prevent the relevant harm occurring, may be criminally liable, with the original act being treated as the Actus Reus. A true omission is where the offence can be categorised in law as one of the following;

There are instances where there is an obligation or a duty to act, these are listed below;

Special Relationship (close familial relationships)

1. Husband and wife

People (DPP) –v- O'Brien[7]; Quirke J held that parties to a marriage owe each other a duty to care even where each spouse is capable of looking after themselves. However, this is not the same duty as is owed to their dependants. The relevant part of Quirke J's judgment reads as follows: "[T]here lies upon a man, who is cohabiting with his wife and who is the mother of his children, a duty to have reasonable care for her health and welfare. Stating that if two people live together as husband and wife they owe a duty to take care of each other.

2. Parent and child

R v Gibbons and Proctor[8]; a child died of starvation after her father and his partner deliberately failed to feed her. Both were convicted of murder on the grounds that the parent's duty towards a young child was so self-evident, his partner had assumed de facto parental (loco parentis) responsibility when she moved in with the family.

Voluntary Assumption of Responsibility

R –v- Stone and Dobinson[9]; Stone and his mistress took Stone's sister into their house to care for her. She had anorexia due to her fears of gaining weight, and because of this she became bedridden. They failed to care for her and she died. The existence of sibling relationships in themselves will not give rise to a

---

[7] People (DPP) v O'Brien (1998)

[8] R v Gibbins and Proctor [1918] 13 Cr App Rep 134

[9] R v. Stone and Dobinson (1977) QB 354

duty of care or duty to act, (***R v Smith***[10] *held that there is no legal obligation on one brother to feed the other*) but the fact that the couple had voluntarily taken her into their home and attempted to care for her by feeding her and attempting to bathe her, they have accepted the responsibility and subsequent duty and liability as an omission. They were charged with manslaughter as they had assumed voluntary responsibility of her.

Where person created the risk

R –v- Miller[11] The defendant was squatting in a building. He lay on a mattress, lit a cigarette and fell asleep. He woke up to find it smouldering, but instead of putting it out, he went to sleep in another room. Miller was convicted of arson as he failed to take measures that lie within one's power, as he himself created the danger. As the fire was his fault, the court treated the Actus Reus of the offence as being his original act of dropping the cigarette and his omission to act after creating the risk.

Where fails duty imposed by contract

R –v- Pitwood[12]; the courts have always been reluctant to impose criminal liability regarding contractual duties due to contracts being private agreements therefore having no legal terms outside of them, Pittwood being the exception to this rule, courts held that whilst the defendants' duty was to his employers, his breach of contract put the public in danger, "a man may incur criminal liability from a duty arising out of contract"

---

[10] R v Smith[1826] 172 ER 203
[11] R v. Miller (1983) 2 AC 161
[12] R v Pittwood [1902] 19 TLR 37

Other types of deaths, which are not normal spontaneous deaths.

Euthanasia

Euthanasia (Greek, "*pleasant death*") means accelerating people's death for some idea of goodness.

Voluntary Euthanasia, the action of a third party, which deliberately ends the life of an individual, with that individual's consent/Euthanasia is illegal in Ireland.

Non-voluntary Euthanasia

Where the individual is unable to ask for euthanasia and another person makes the decision on his/her behalf, usually based on previously expressed wishes.

This includes cases where:

- the person is in a coma
- the person is too young (e.g. a very the young baby)
- the person is senile
- the person is mentally retarded to a very severe extent
- the person is severely brain-damaged
- the person is mentally disturbed in such a way that they should be protected from themselves" *

Assisted Suicide

Where an individual takes his/her own life based on information, guidance and/or medication provided by a third party.

Physician Assisted Suicide

Where a doctor provides the information, guidance and/or medication with which an individual can take his/her own life.

Abortion

An abortion is the physical process of ending a pregnancy and expelling the foetus before it has fully developed in the womb. Depending on the gestation period of the foetus and the health of the mother, the process can be completed using medications or surgical means.

Infanticide

Infanticide or infant homicide is the killing of a human infant in the first year of life. Neonaticide, a killing within 24 hours of a baby's birth, is most commonly done by the mother. Infanticide was carried out through the ages, even as far back as King Herod, who ordered the deaths of all first-born males to societies who kill female infants in gender selection. Some societies killed disabled babies in order to alleviate the strain of raising these babies.

Chapter 4

Theft, Burglary, Aggravated Burglary and Robbery

Section 4 of the Criminal Justice Act 2001

Section 4 (6) of the Criminal Justice (Theft and Fraud Offences) Act, 2001 provides:

4.—(1) Subject to section 5 , a person is guilty of theft if he or she dishonestly appropriates property without the consent of its owner and with the intention of depriving its owner of it.

(2) For the purposes of this section a person does not appropriate property without the consent of its owner if—

(a) the person believes that he or she has the owner's consent, or would have the owner's consent if the owner knew of the appropriation of the property and the circumstances in which it was appropriated, or

(b) (except where the property came to the person as trustee or personal representative) he or she appropriates the property in the belief that the owner cannot be discovered by taking reasonable steps, but consent obtained by deception or intimidation is not consent for those purposes.

(3) (a) This subsection applies to a person who, in the course of business, holds property in trust for, or on behalf of, more than one owner.

(b) Where a person to whom this subsection applies appropriates some of the property so held to his or her own use or benefit, the person shall, for the purposes of subsection (1) but subject to subsection (2), be deemed to have appropriated the property or, as the case may be, a sum representing it without the consent of its owner or owners.

(c) If in any proceedings against a person to whom this subsection applies for theft of some or all of the property so held by him or her it is proved that—

(i) there is a deficiency in the property or a sum representing it, and

(ii) the person has failed to provide a satisfactory explanation for the whole or any part of the deficiency, it shall be presumed, until the contrary is proved, for the purposes of subsection (1) but subject to subsection (2), that the person appropriated, without the consent of its owner or owners, the whole or that part of the deficiency.

(4) If at the trial of a person for theft the court or jury, as the case may be, has to consider whether the person believed—

(a) that he or she had not acted dishonestly, or

(b) that the owner of the property concerned had consented or would have consented to its appropriation, or

(c) that the owner could not be discovered by taking reasonable steps,

the presence or absence of reasonable grounds for such a belief is a matter to which the court or jury shall have regard, in conjunction with any other relevant matters, in considering whether the person so believed.

(5) In this section—

"appropriates", in relation to property, means usurps or adversely interferes with the proprietary rights of the owner of the property;

"depriving" means temporarily or permanently depriving.

(6) A person guilty of theft is liable on conviction on indictment to a fine or imprisonment for a term not exceeding 10 years or both.

Theft is "an arrestable offence".

"an arrestable offence" was defined in the Criminal Law Act 1997 as an offence for which a person of full capacity and not previously convicted may, under or by virtue of any enactment, be punished by imprisonment for a term of five years or by a more severe penalty and includes an attempt to commit any such offence;"

Actus Reus and Mens Rea of theft

Most crimes comprise two elements, an Actus Reus ('guilty act') and a Mens Rea ('guilty mind'). *Actus non facitreum nisi mens sit rea.* ', **"An act does not make a man guilty of a crime, unless his mind be also guilty."**

You cannot have a crime unless the guilty mind and act are present together at the same time.

All crimes require proof of an Actus Reus. Furthermore, there is a presumption that each part of the Actus Reus requires proof of a corresponding Mens Rea. Offences to which the presumption of Mens Rea does not apply are called crimes of strict liability.

4.—(1) Subject to section 5 , a person is guilty of theft if he or she dishonestly appropriates property without the consent of its owner and with the intention of depriving its owner of it.

Actus Reus *of Theft is appropriating property without consent of the owner,*

Mens Rea *of Theft is the intention of depriving the owner of the property.*

Theft, robbery and burglary.

Theft is 'the dishonest appropriation of property belonging to another with the intention of permanently depriving that person of it'.

Put simply this means taking someone else's property intending it will not be returned. There needs to be an element of dishonesty present. If someone believes they have a right to take property or the owner would have consented, this could mean a theft has not been committed.

For example, *a person goes into your garden shed and removes your lawn mower, they take the lawn mower to a hiding place, and then advertise it for sale, they sell it and use the money to buy themselves a new outfit, and this is removing property belonging to another with the intention of permanently depriving them of it.*

Specific thefts such as electricity and gas

Abstracting electricity (or gas) contrary to **section 15(2)(a) of the Energy (Miscellaneous Provisions) Act, 1995**

(a) A person who dishonestly uses, or causes to be wasted or diverted, any electricity or gas shall be guilty of an offence.

(b) For the purposes of this subsection an act is done by a person dishonestly if the person does the act without claim of legal right.

*(**Example:** Particulars of Offence - A. B., on (or about) the ... day of ... 20 at (place) in the County of ..., dishonestly used (or caused to be wasted or diverted) electricity (or gas).*

Unlawful interference contrary to **section 15(3) of the Energy (Miscellaneous Provisions) Act, 1995.**

A person who unlawfully interferes with any article owned by or, under the control of, the Electricity Supply Board or Bord Gáis Eireann shall be guilty of an offence. **Boggeln v Williams (1978) QBD**

Theft - dishonesty - abstracting electricity

The defendant failed to pay a bill and was disconnected. Then, the Defendant told an employee of the Electricity Board that he intended to reconnect the supply - he did this through the meter so that they would know how much electricity he used.

He was charged with abstracting electricity

Held: the Defendant's belief in his own honesty was crucial. Sec 13 did not make taking of electricity without due authority dishonest. Not Guilty.

Robbery

Robbery is the taking or attempting to take anything of value by force, threat of force, or by putting the victim in fear.

a) Robbery is where 'a person steals and immediately before or at the time and in order to do so, uses force on any person or puts or seeks to put, any person in fear of being, then and there, subjected to force'.

Basically, robbery involves violence or the threat of violence and something being stolen. **For example**, *someone is approached in the street, knocked to the ground and their wallet or handbag is stolen.*

b) It is also robbery to be approached by someone, threatened with a knife or similar weapon and have the offender property taken.
c) Robbery can take many forms ranging from a street mugging as described above, to an armed robbery of a bank.

It is not uncommon for people to say 'My house has been robbed' when they actually mean they have been burgled. Unless a degree of violence is used or threatened, it is NOT robbery. ***Coffey, R v (1987) CA   Theft – intention to permanently deprive***

Did they rob it? Should the defendant remove property from another with the intention of returning it and not permanently depriving them of it then the jury might find the defendant not guilty where they can prove they merely intended to borrow it.

Burglary under section 12 of the Criminal Justice Act 2001

Burglary, a person commits burglary if he enters a building, or any part of a building, as a trespasser, with intent to either:

- steal anything in the building,
- inflict GBH on any person in the building
- or doing unlawful damage...

This basically means that having entered any building, or part of a building as a trespasser, the person is guilty of an offence if they steal, attempt to steal, inflict grievous bodily harm, or attempt to commit grievous bodily harm to another.

12.—(1) A person is guilty of burglary if he or she—

(a) enters any building or part of a building as a trespasser and with intent to commit an arrestable offence, or

(b) having entered any building or part of a building as a trespasser, commits or attempts to commit any such offence therein.

(2) References in subsection (1) to a building shall apply also to an inhabited vehicle or vessel and to any other inhabited temporary or movable structure, and shall apply to any such vehicle, vessel or structure at times when the person having a habitation in it is not there as well as at times when the person is there.

(3) A person guilty of burglary is liable on conviction on indictment to a fine or imprisonment for a term not exceeding 14 years or both.

(4) In this section, "arrestable offence" means an offence for which a person of full age and not previously convicted may be punished by imprisonment for a term of five years or by a more severe penalty.

'Enter' as a 'Trespasser' – **there must be an entry** (be substantially or wholly inside the building, not merely attempting to enter) - **the entry must be trespass** (enter land or property without permission)

The Actus Reus of Burglary- Is the entry of a building as a trespasser.

The Mens Rea of the ulterior offence has to be proved, in addition to intentional or reckless trespass. So for example, theft requires proof of dishonesty and intention to deprive

Aggravated burglary s. 13 the Criminal Justice Act 2001

The elements of burglary referred to above have application to aggravated burglary. The additional elements are that at the time an suspect has with him any firearm or imitation firearm, any weapon of offence or any explosive. It is provided by section 13(1) that:

A person is guilty of aggravated burglary if he or she commits any burglary and at the time has with him or her any firearm or imitation firearm, any weapon of offence or any explosive.

"firearm or imitation firearm", "weapon of offence" "explosive".

These terms are as defined in section 13(2): "explosive" means any article manufactured for the purpose of producing a practical effect by explosion, or intended by the person having it with him or her for that purpose; "firearm" means:

(a) a lethal firearm or other lethal weapon of any description from which any shot, bullet or other missile can be discharged,

(b) an air gun (which expression includes an air rifle and an air pistol) or any other weapon incorporating a barrel from which metal or other slugs can be discharged,

(c) a crossbow,

(d) any type of stun gun or other weapon for causing any shock or other disablement to a person by means of electricity or any other kind of energy emission; "imitation firearm" means anything which is not a firearm but has the appearance of being one;

"weapon of offence" means:

(a) any article which has a blade or sharp point,

(b) any other article made or adapted for use for causing injury to or incapacitating a person, or intended by the person having it with him or her for such use or for threatening such use,

(c) any weapon of whatever description designed for the discharge of any noxious liquid, noxious gas or other noxious thing. Handcuffs are an example of an article made for incapacitation, and a piece of rope would be if it was intended that it would be used to tie a person up.

In **Kelly (1992),** it was held that the suspect who had used a screwdriver to effect an entry, became guilty of aggravated burglary when he used it to prod a person in the stomach.

"at the time"

"at the time" for a person to be convicted, it is necessary to show that he had the firearm etc. with him at the time he committed the burglary. In the case of 12(1)(a) "at the time" is the time of entry, in the case of 12(1)(b) "at the time" is at the time of commission of the arrestable offence.

In **Francis (1982),** the suspect gained entry to a house, armed with sticks. After throwing away the sticks he stole property. The Court of Appeal substituted a conviction for burglary for one of aggravated burglary. Unless the suspect intended to steal when he entered the house, he was only guilty of aggravated burglary if he had a weapon with him at the time when he stole.

In **O'Leary (1986),** the suspect entered a house as a trespasser, took a knife from the kitchen and went upstairs and used the knife to force the occupier to hand over property. It was held by the Court of Appeal that the material time for the possession of a weapon is the point at which the suspect actually stole.

Penalty s. 13(3) the Criminal Justice Act 2001

A person guilty of aggravated burglary is liable on conviction on indictment to imprisonment for life.

Section 14 Criminal Justice Act 2001

14.—(1) A person is guilty of robbery if he or she steals, and immediately before or at the time of doing so, and in order to do so, uses force on any person or puts or seeks to put any person in fear of being then and there subjected to force.

(2) A person guilty of robbery is liable on conviction on indictment to imprisonment for life.

Actus Reus = 3 Main elements. Same as theft plus force

(a) Stealing;

(b) Using force; or

(c) Fear of force being used.

Mens Rea = same as theft

In *R v Robinson,* the defendant threatened the victim with a knife in order to recover money which he was actually owed. His conviction for robbery was quashed on the basis that Robinson had an honest, although unreasonable, belief in his legal right to the money.

In **R v Hale (1978)** the application of force and the stealing took place in different locations, and it was not possible to establish the timing; it was held that the appropriation necessary to prove theft was a continuing act, and the jury could correctly convict of robbery.

Chapter 5

Defences to a Crime

The purposes of a defence to a crime

In a criminal case, the Director of Public Prosecutions (DPP) must prove **_beyond a reasonable doubt_** that the suspect had the actus reus and mens rea to commit a crime. The suspect has a legal right to put forward a defence, the defence can be any of the following:

1.   Deny committing the act; disputing the actus reus. *"I didn't do it"*
2.   Argue they lacked intent; disputing the mens rea. *"I did it, but I was too drunk to know what I was doing."*
3.   Attempt to justify why they committed the act. *"I did it, but I was defending myself from attack."*

Not every criminal act is or should be followed by a criminal conviction, say for instance a person was attacked and during that attach the push of the suspect, knocking them to the ground and causing them to bang their heads and die, it would not be in societies best interest to send the victim to prison, as they were merely defending themselves.

A fundamental reason why the criminal law contains a number of defences is because it is not a tool for vengeance, but is one of the means of attempting to ensure the peaceful co-existence of citizens inside a community.[13]

The defence of Infancy

Infancy is a criminal defence, descended from old British common law that attempts to challenge liability for a crime because of the defendant's very young age. Originally common law assumed that young children were incapable of the intent (*mens rea*) needed to commit a criminal act, the Common law infancy defence traditionally halts the prosecution of children under the age of seven for crimes and presumptively precludes the prosecution of children aged seven to fourteen years under the adult criminal law system.

The infancy defence operates under the idea (on the basis) that children cannot be prosecuted as adults because they lack the emotional and cognitive maturity

---

[13] http://www.lawreform.ie/_fileupload/reports/rdefencesincriminallaw.pdf

to understand the moral nature of their actions. At common law, children under the age of seven were held to be doli incapax,

"doli incapax": children of 10 (up to 10 years of age) are considered too the offender to be liable at all for crimes they commit *(S.52 of the Children Act 2001)*, ***KM v. DPP [1994] 1 IR 514*** or irrebuttably *(no evidence is capable of disproving)* incapable of forming criminal intent, while children between seven and fourteen years old were presumed such, though this presumption *(belief "on probability")* might be rebutted *(proven wrong)* if very strong evidence was presented to show that the child held a moral understanding of his actions.

The purpose of criminal law is that of fair, just legal system, and the courts were not assembled to punish children so young as not to know what they were doing. On the other hand the courts had to ensure that children were not carrying out crime knowing they would get away with them. The important factors in determining if a child was found guilty was, whether the child understood the nature of his/her conduct.

However, in modern times this presumption is being challenged as children are more self-aware and the courts are finding criminal intent in young children, more and more cases of youth offenders being sent to adult courts for trial.

The defence of Intoxication

Self-induced intoxication can be raised as a defence to crimes of specific intent, but not to crimes of basic intent. **General rule** - if a person is voluntarily intoxicated and commits a crime the defence may be used as a partial defence only to crimes requiring specific intent. If successful, this defence can lower a conviction or reduce a criminal sentence. Basic intent cases cannot use this as a defence.

- ***Murder is Specific Intent;***
- ***Manslaughter on the other hand is Basic Intent.***

Example: If an intoxicated person severely assault a victim, and they avoid being charged with aggravated assault because they did not endanger the person's life knowingly (specific intent), but the accused may still be convicted of a lesser assault charge (general intent). It was stressed in R ***v Sheehan and Moore [1975] 1 WLR 739***, that "a drunken intent is nevertheless an intent".

The effect of intoxication on criminal liability is well-established in the UK jurisdiction. In **DPP v Majewski**, the House of Lords held that evidence of intoxication could negate specific intent but that it would not absolve a suspect of liability for a crime of basic intent. While that decision has been much criticised and has been departed from in several jurisdictions, the CCA (Court of Criminal Appeal) confirmed that it represents Irish law and that a change could only be effected by legislation.

In **People (DPP) v Reilly,** the applicant, who was convicted of manslaughter, had argued that he was in a state of automatism at the time of the killing. Relying on Majewski, the trial judge ruled that automatism brought about by the voluntary consumption of alcohol did not afford a defence and that while murder required proof of specific intent, the offence of manslaughter did not. This ruling was approved by the CCA:

Intoxication by Drugs

If a person consciously and deliberately takes drugs not on medical prescription, but in order to escape from reality, to "go on a trip" or to become hallucinated, he cannot plead his self-induced disability as a defence to a **basic intent crime**

The Burden of Proof

The burden rests on the defendant to provide some evidence of intoxication which can be put before the jury; the onus will then be on the prosecution to establish beyond all reasonable doubt that, although such evidence exists, the defendant still had the necessary Mens Rea.

Burden Of Proof and Defences

The proposition established in People **(DPP) v Davis** that the suspect bears an evidential burden in relation to provocation, has been extended to cases of self-defence.

In reaching this conclusion in **O'Carroll v DPP**, the *CCA noted that the evidential burden is not heavy. The burden involves the suspect's being able to point to some evidence that suggests the presence of the elements of the defence. The trial judge must be satisfied that "an issue of substance, as distinct from a contrived issue or a vague possibility" has been raised. *Court of Criminal Appeal

Defence of Mistake

A suspect can put forward mistake as a defence, this defence shows a lack of mens rea due to an honest mistake. **Note:** Ignorance of the facts, or not understanding all of the details of a situation, can be used as a defence. However, ignorance of the law, or not knowing a particular offence was illegal, is no defence.

Example: *A person is out shopping and is given fake money in change, this person then goes to another shop and buys goods, this suspect knows that counterfeit or fake money is illegal, but they had no idea they themselves were using fake*

Ignorance of the law is no defence *"Ignorantia juris non excusat"* is a well know principle, this is also set out in the case of DPP v Morgan, which stated that ignorance of the law is no excuse

A mistake of fact will suffice provided the mistake was such as to prevent the defendant forming the Mens Rea of the offence. Whilst initially the mistake was required to be both honest and reasonably held, in DPP v Morgan it was held that the mistake need only be honest. There was no requirement that it was reasonable for the defendant to make the mistake: **DPP v Morgan [1976] A.C. 182**

Defence of Insanity

People in Ireland who are charged with a criminal offence and who are suffering from a mental disorder are dealt with under ***the Criminal Law (Insanity) Act 2010***.

The question of the mental state of someone in Ireland charged with a crime may arise at two different stages - at the start of the trial and at the decision on guilt. If a person is suffering from a mental disorder, they may be considered unfit to be tried at the start of the trial. In that case, no trial takes place. If a trial is held and the person is considered to have actually committed the offence but was insane at the time, it is possible for a verdict of not guilty by reason of insanity to be reached. In murder cases, the concept of diminished responsibility may be used to substitute a verdict of manslaughter.

A mental disorder in Irish law is defined as including mental illness, mental disability, dementia or any disease of the mind but does not include intoxication (drunkenness).

Fit or unfit to be tried

The decision on whether or not a person is fit to be tried is made by a judge. If the person cannot understand the charge or is unable to instruct a legal team, challenge jurors or follow the evidence, then they may be considered unfit to be tried.

This finding (that is, that someone is considered unfit to be tried) is not a decision on the alleged criminal activity. If someone is found to be unfit to be tried, then the trial is postponed. The judge then decides what happens next. For example, the person may be committed to a psychiatric hospital or unit if they are considered to be suffering from a mental disorder and are in need of in-patient treatment under the terms of **the Mental Health Act, 2001**. Alternatively, the person may be sent for out-patient psychiatric care. The person may be committed to a psychiatric hospital or unit for 14 days in order to establish whether or not they should be sent for treatment. The person may appeal against a committal order.

If the judge considers that there is a reasonable doubt that the person committed the alleged crime, the person may be acquitted. The Director of Public Prosecutions may appeal against a decision that a person is unfit to be tried.

Not guilty by reason of insanity

If someone is considered to have actually committed the offence but was insane at the time, the verdict may be not guilty by reason of insanity. This decision is made by a jury. If this verdict is reached, the judge may order that the person be committed to a psychiatric hospital or unit in broadly the same way as applies in the case of being unfit to be tried.

Diminished responsibility in murder cases

If someone is charged with murder, the verdict of not guilty by reason of insanity is one possible verdict. **_The Criminal Law (Insanity) Act 2010_** provides for the concept of diminished responsibility in murder cases. A conviction for murder in Ireland brings an automatic life sentence. In other crimes, the judge has discretion in relation to sentencing and so can take into account any diminished responsibility which may exist. If someone charged with murder successfully pleads diminished responsibility, then the verdict is manslaughter. The judge can then sentence the person to any length of time in prison.

The M'Naghten Rules

Prior to the M'Naghten Rules being in place the "insane" were not held responsible for their actions. Ancient Hebrew laws stated that "idiots, lunatics, and children" are unable to tell the difference between good and evil thus relieving them of responsibility for their actions (Maeder, 1985).

However, starting with the 13th century in England, more cases dealing with the "insane" were being dealt with. The test for whether or not these people were "insane" was really up to whoever was king at the time. Over time it shifted to looking at the person on trial and then other people would use their human judgement to determine whether or not they were able to tell good from evil (Weinreb, 1986).

Daniel M'Naghten

In1843 when the public was outraged that Daniel M'Naghten was acquitted of his charges for his attempted assassination of the Prime Minister (*accidentally shooting the Secretary to the Prime Minister whom he mistook for the Prime Minister of England at the time, Robert Peel*) because he was deemed "insane" and because of this he was found not guilty, which caused outcry, due to this the Central Criminal Court was instructed to define what "insanity" actually was. One of the judges answered:

> "in all cases that every man is to be presumed to be sane...until the contrary be proved...and that to establish a defence on the ground of insanity, it must be clearly proved that, at the time of the committing of the act, the party suspect was labouring under such a defect of reason, from disease of the mind, as not to know the nature and quality of the act he was doing; or if he did know it, that he did not know he was doing what was wrong"

This very answer was what became the M'Naghten rule or rules

Most common law countries used this rule, however it was criticised by many in the legal fields as insufficient in the determination of insanity, there were there areas which legal theorists believed it failed:

- the rule is not in accord with psychiatric knowledge
- the rule does not permit complete and adequate testimony

- the psychiatric expert testifying under the rule does not make a scientific contribution but assumes the role of ethical judge

Ever since 1943, the M'Naghten rule has been the standard test of criminal responsibility when applied to the defence of insanity. "To establish a defence on the ground of insanity, it must be clearly proved that, at the time of the committing of the act, the party suspect was labouring under such a defect of reason, from disease of the mind, as not to know the nature and quality of the act he was doing; or if he did know it, that he did not know he was doing what was wrong". "Disease of the mind" is a wide-ranging concept which is capable of encompassing all forms of mental disorder which give rise to a 'defect of reason'.

Defence of Automatism

Automatism is an involuntary action by a person who cannot control their actions and who is in a state of impaired consciousness.

1. Automatism can be divided into two types:– **insane** *and* **non-insane**
2. Various factors can influence "automatic" behaviour, from sleepwalking, the consumption of drugs and alcohol, to a disease of the mind.

Although the conduct element of the Actus Reus of an offence usually requires proof of a positive act on the part of the defendant, some offences can be committed by virtue of an omission to act.

The Court of Criminal Appeal in Northern Ireland considered that automatism meant the state of a person who, though capable of action, is not conscious of what he is doing. It means unconscious involuntary action, and it is a defence because the mind does not go with the action which is being done.

Lord Denning in the case of **Bratty v Attorney General for Northern Ireland [1961] 3 All ER 523 HL** said:

"No act is punishable if it is done involuntarily and an involuntary act in this context: some people nowadays prefer to speak of it as `automatism' – which means, an act which is done by the muscles without any control by the mind such as a spasm, a reflex action or a convulsion; or an act done by a person who is not conscious of what he is doing, such as an act done whilst suffering from concussion or whilst sleep- walking.

Insane automatism

Every man is presumed to be sane, and to possess a sufficient degree of   reason to be responsible for his crimes until the contrary is proved.   **M'Naghten (1843)**

Insanity is one of the exceptions to the rule of Automatism. This type of automatism is linked to a mental illness. • If it can be proven that a suspect suffered from a mental illness and as a result was incapable of knowing that what they were doing was wrong, the suspect may be declared not criminally responsible and referred for psychiatric treatment.

Example*: a person with paranoid schizophrenia leaves home and sees a person they (wrongly) believe to be a threat to them and murder them, because of their mental illness, and if they cannot understand the implications of their actions, they may be found not guilty by reason of insanity.*

It is the M'Naghten rules which set out the defence of insanity. Suspects will be acquitted if they can prove that when committed the crime, they were legally insane. For the defence to succeed, it must be proved that, at the time of the offence, the defendant was suffering from a mental illness causing them to be unaware of their actions, or the severity or impact of their actions, or that their actions were wrong. A defendant does not have to be in a state of automatism to be deemed insane within the M'Naghten rules.

- It is the part of the rule that the defect of reason be 'caused by a disease of the mind' which is at issue in cases concerning automatism.
- Although medical evidence is essential here, insanity is a legal concept, not a medical one.
- It is a question of law and it follows that it is for the judge to rule whether the condition the defendant was suffering from constitutes a 'disease of the mind' and therefore insanity.
- Therefore, although the defendant must raise medical evidence as to his condition, 'insanity' is a legal concept and not a medical one.

Some conditions such as hyperglycaemia (high blood sugar), sleepwalking and epilepsy have been held to be diseases of the mind for the purpose of distinguishing between sane and insane automatism.

Constrained Choice

Most common law systems stress the element of constrained choice as the conceptual or theoretical basis for the defences of duress and necessity. Emphasis on the element of constrained choice highlights the gravamen or inner nature of the defendant's predicament, while at the same time underlining the essential difference between the pleas of necessity and duress and those of physical coercion or force majeure.

In a situation of physical coercion the defendant has no choice; as would be true, for example, where he causes the death of a pedestrian as a result of his car being blown off course by a sudden storm. In contrast, in situations of duress and necessity the defendant faces a moral dilemma. Through no fault of his own, he is placed in the difficult predicament of having to choose between abiding by the law and becoming a victim of violence, or breaking the law in order to protect himself or another from the threat of serious assault or mortal danger.

The best-known example of duress in Irish law arose in ***Attorney General v Whelan***. There the defendant admitted that he had knowingly received stolen property, but claimed that he acted under pressure of serious threats. The Court of Criminal Appeal held that he was entitled to the defence of duress in these circumstances and set out the essential conditions of the plea in Irish law. If successful, the plea of duress affords a complete defence.

Defence of Necessity

Necessity can come about when the suspect claims they were forced to commit a criminal act because they were in danger themselves. ***R –v- Dudley and Stephens***

The Courts have ruled that this defence may only be used in situations where there appears to be "imminent risk." • **Example**: A woman is in labour and her partner speeds to the hospital to ensure she doesn't deliver in the car, they are stopped on the way by a police officer who charges them with speeding, they can argue the defence of necessity to ensure she got to hospital safe.

Defence of Duress

The defence of duress can be used when a suspect says they did something illegal because someone threatened or coerced them to do it, and this was against his or her will. •

Duress is similar to the necessity defence; in both defences the suspect claims to have been forced to commit a crime as the result of being in imminent danger. • The main difference is that with duress the accused is **_forced_** to act as the result of a threat.

Example: *Mike shoots Sadie and tells Andy that he must help him dump the body. When Andy refuses, Mike points his gun at him, which compels Andy to cooperate.*

The only Irish case which has examined the nature and scope of the defence of duress is the 1933 decision of the Court of Criminal Appeal in **Attorney General v Whelan.**

The defendant was charged with having received a sum of stolen money, knowing it to be stolen. He had also been indicted, with others, on a charge of conspiracy to steal a quantity of money from a train but was found not guilty on the conspiracy charge. Another man, Farnan, had also been indicted on the conspiracy charge and had pleaded guilty. Farnan had brought a box of coins which had been stolen in the train robbery to the defendant's house late one night. The defendant admitted he had accepted the money but said that he had done so under duress from Farnan, who was armed with a revolver.

During the trial the judge stated; there was no doubt that Farnan was the type of man to threaten to use a revolver, if not actually use it, he told the jury to decide if it was duress or not, he asked the question **"[I]n receiving the money did Peter Whelan act under threats of immediate death or serious personal violence?"**

The jury stated they agreed he acted in duress, however, the judge then ruled that the defence was in mitigating and not defence. On appeal to the Court of Criminal Appeal, the defendant agreed that the finding of the jury that he had acted under duress and this amounted to a not guilty verdict.

Defence of Coercion

Coercion is the intimidation of a victim to compel him or her to do some act against his or her will by the use of psychological pressure, physical force, or threats.

The crime of intentionally and unlawfully restraining another's freedom by threatening to commit a crime, accusing the victim of a crime, disclosing any secret that would seriously impair the victim's reputation in the community, or by performing or refusing to perform an official action lawfully requested by the victim, or by causing an official to do so can be defined as coercion.

A defence asserted in a criminal prosecution that a person who committed a crime did not do so of his or her own free will, but only because the individual was compelled by another through the use of physical force or threat of immediate serious bodily injury or death.

Defence of Provocation

Charleton, in his book **"concession to human frailty",** he defined provocation as "Sudden and temporary loss of self-control." When a person is "provoked", they can be defined as having lost their self-control, and as a result they commit a crime.

It must be noted that Provocation can only be used as a partial defence to justify the actions of the accused. They will not be found innocent under this defence, but heir sentence may be reduced. *The People (DPP) –v- MacEoin*

Example: Sam and his Wife Emma are at a bar, when Jack approaches them and starts to insult Emma, Sam is so angry at this person for insulting his wife that he hits him and breaks his nose, Sam can use the defence of provocation and claim that if jack had not insulted Emma the Sam would never have hit him.

Self-Defence

Self-Defence can be used as a defence; it is the legal use of reasonable force in order to defend yourself and your property. *The People (DPP) –v- Nally* •

The Criminal Law (Defence and the Dwelling) Act 2011 allows people to use force if they have to defend themselves or their property, but the amount of force should not be excessive; no more than necessary. It must be noted that the use or exchange of force must be reasonable.

Example: *A person being attacked with a weapon may use a weapon to defend him- or herself. But they cannot go looking for a gun to defend their property of the suspect has no weapon. (You can't bring a gun to a knife fight)*

Entrapment

This is a little used or should I say little "successful" defence in Ireland. <u>*Syon v Hewitt & McTiernan [2006]*</u> (Tobacco control officers sent underage person into a shop to buy cigarettes which the defendant sold) It can be defined as a Gardai's/Officers action induces a person to commit a crime. If a Garda coerces or forces a person to commit a crime, the officer is guilty of entrapment. • If the accused can prove the Garda/Officer led them to participate in a crime, the court can dismiss the charges immediately.

Example: *Monika is continually encouraged by an undercover garda to purchase illegal drugs. If Monika can convince the court that she would not have purchased drugs without the undercover officer's forceful encouragement, she can claim the officer "entrapped" her.*

Conclusion

This booklet introduced you to the general principles of criminal responsibility and to a selection of substantive criminal offences and also criminal defences as well. The substantive offences include assault, theft, murder, manslaughter, and property offences, whilst the criminal defences including insanity and self-defence. There are many other areas of Criminal law which are used in both charging an offender and defending the suspect, I have used the basic rules and basic criminal offences and defences in this booklet, if you require in-depth research into criminal procedures, charges or defences in Ireland please see below a list of recommended reading for Criminal law in Ireland.

By now I would hope that you will have the knowledge and skills to:

1. Identify, explain and apply the principles of criminal law covered in the booklet;
2. Access, use, interpret and apply complex statutory material to solve criminal law problems
3. Select and apply critical thinking required to bring about solutions to complex criminal law problems and/or issues in the context of individual and collaborative problem solving.

An Introduction to Criminal Law in Ireland

Criminal Law Quiz

Types of Offences

Summary: _____

Examples: _____

Indictable: _____

Examples: _____

Hybrid: _____

Examples: _____

Elements of Crime

Mens Rea : _____

Actus Reus: _____

Ireland's justice system is based on the _____ System.

This means:

_____

Factors:

Aggravating: _____

Examples: _____

Mitigating: _____

Examples: _____

An Introduction to Criminal Law in Ireland

Elements of a Crime:

In order for a person to be convicted of a crime, the _____ must prove that _____ existed at the time that the offence was committed.

_____ + _____ = _____

Actus Reus: "_____." As defined in _____

- This can be an _____, or an _____ or a _____.

- Must be shown that the person committed an act _____ by _____.

- Failure to do something (example: for parents to withhold the necessities of life for their children)

Mens Rea – "_____"

- Mens rea is the technical term for the blameworthy _____ of _____ that must be proven beyond a _____ doubt by the _____.

1. _____ – the true _____ of the act. Carrying out a criminal act while being aware what the results will be and ignoring the _____.

Example: bringing a weapon to a robbery

- _____- intent is limited to the act itself. Committing a wrongful act with no _____ _____.

Example: hitting someone because you are angry

- _____- when the person committing the offence has a further criminal _____. Committing a wrongful act in order to _____ another.

Example: hitting someone because you want to steal something from him.

An Introduction to Criminal Law in Ireland

- The law considers some people incapable of forming intent: i.e.

    - _____,

    - _____,

    - _____

2. _____- knowledge of _____ – prove *mens rea*

    - _____- reason for committing an offence

        - Not the same as intent

        - Does not establish guilt of the accused

        - Can be used as circumstantial (indirect) evidence

3. _____ - _____ disregard for the possible result of an _____.

        - People don't intend to harm others however they understand the _____ of their actions and proceed anyway.

Example: taking prescription drugs that you know make you drowsy and then operating a motor vehicle

4. _____ - doing something or _____ to do something with "_____ disregard for the lives or _____ of other persons"

Example: throwing a beer bottle out of a moving vehicle and injuring someone

5. _____ - turning a _____ eye to the _____ of your action

Example: buying stolen property that you should know has been stolen

An Introduction to Criminal Law in Ireland

Match each term with the correct statement below:

a. automatism   f. not criminally responsible

b. alibi   g. ignorance of the law

c. necessity   h. defence

d. duress   i. entrapment

e. provocation   j. non-insane automatism

Fill in the Blanks (from above)

1. ____   an involuntary state of mind

2. ____   a formulated response to criminal charges

3. ____   not an accepted defence

4. ___   a defence when the accused was forced to commit a
                    crime because of certain danger

5. ____   the best defence possible

6. ____   a defence to a crime committed in the "heat of passion"

7. ____   being forced to commit a crime by external pressure

8. ____   a result of mental disease

9. ____   a defence related to external factors such as
                    sleepwalking

10. ____   coercion by the police to commit a crime

"I want to live perfectly above the law, and make it my servant, instead of my master." ~ Brigham young

Recommended Reading

Ashworth, Principles of Criminal Law, 6th ed. (Oxford University Press, 2009)

Campbell, Kilcommins and O'Sullivan, Criminal Law in Ireland: Cases and Commentaries (Dublin, 2009).

Charleton, McDermott and Bolger, Criminal law (Dublin, 1999)

C Wells & O Quick, Lacey, Wells and Quick Reconstructing Criminal Law: Text and Materials(4th edn, Cambridge2010)

Hanly, An Introduction to Irish Criminal Law 2nd ed. (Dublin, 2006)

Herring, Criminal Law: Text, Cases and Materials 4th ed (Oxford University Press, 2010).

McIntyre, McMullan and O Toghda, Criminal Law (Dublin, 2012)

McAuley and McCutcheon, Criminal liability: A Grammar (Dublin, 2000).

Ormerod, Smith and Hogan Criminal Law, 13th ed. (Oxford University Press, 2011).

O'Malley, Sexual Offences 2nd ed. (Dublin, 2013).

McGreal, Criminal Justice (Theft and Fraud Offences) Act, 2001 (Annotated Statute) (2nd ed., Dublin, 2011).

References:

Ashworth, Principles of Criminal Law, 6th ed. (Oxford University Press, 2009)

Bloomsbury Professional - J.C.W. Wylie. 1999. Irish Conveyancing Statutes. [ONLINE] Available at: http://www.bloomsburyprofessionalonline.com/view/irish-conveyancing-statutes/ICS-cases-UID7.xml. [Accessed 01 February 16].

Campbell, Kilcommins and O'Sullivan, Criminal Law in Ireland: Cases and Commentaries (Dublin, 2009).

C Wells & O Quick, Lacey, Wells and Quick Reconstructing Criminal Law: Text and Materials(4th edn, Cambridge2010)

Citizen Information, C. o. (2011). Classification of Crime. Retrieved 2013, from Citizens Information: 1. http://www.citizensinformation.ie/en/justice/criminal_law/criminal_offences/classific ation_of_crimes_in_criminal_cases.html

Classification of Offences. (2011). Retrieved 2012, from Citizens Information: http://www.citizensinformation.ie/en/justice/criminal_law/criminal_offences/classific ation_of_crimes_in_criminal_cases.html

Citizens Information (2010) [online], available from http://www.citizensinformation.ie/en/ [accessed 2 June 2011].

Clyne, T (2014) Business law in Ireland, Oiliuna, Dublin

Clyne, T (2015) An Introduction to the Irish Legal System; Retrieved 2014; http://teresaclyne.com/

Contract e-book. 2013. Contract e-book. [ONLINE] Available at: http://legalmax.info/conbook/index.htm#t=atlas_ex.htm. [Accessed 10 May 15].

Contract Law; 2007; Paul A. McDermott (Butterworths) as referenced @. Mason Hayes and Curran. [ONLINE] Available at: http://www.google.ie/url?sa=t&rct=j&q=&esrc=s&source=web&cd=6&cad=rja&uact=8 &ved=0ahUKEwjZgfTstdbKAhUCdw8KHYadDHQQFghHMAU&url=http%3A%2F%2Fww w.mhc.ie%2Fuploads%2FChange_in_privity_of_contract_rules_230107.pdf&usg=AFQjC NFMc5Z32OO997PIQE5XonkobTTSUQ&sig2=2BMsBXO5FD2usejmak9Y6Q&bvm=bv.1 13034660,d.ZWU. [Accessed 03 February 16].

Elaw Cases. 2010. ElawResources. [ONLINE] Available at: http://e-lawresources.co.uk/cases/Schawel-v-Reade.php. [Accessed 01 November 15].

E-law Resources. 2013. Contract Law Duress. [ONLINE] Available at: http://www.e-lawresources.co.uk/North-Ocean-Shipping-v-Hyundai-Construction-%28The-Atlantic-Baron%29.php. [Accessed 01 February 16].

Dave M. (n.d.). President labelled a 'little midget parasite'. A protest too far? Retrieved 2 2, 2012, from Politics.ie: http://www.politics.ie/forum/current-affairs/234280-president-labelled-little-midget-parasite-protest-too-far-108.html

Didimus. (2007, May). Congratulations to atheist.ie for international publicity success. Retrieved 2012, from Politics.ie: http://www.politics.ie/forum/current-affairs/121513-congratulations-atheist-ie-international-publicity-success-34.html

Elawresources, M. (2009). Thorne v Motor Trade Association [1937] AC 797. Retrieved 2012, from Elawrescources.co.uk: http://e-lawresources.co.uk/Thorne-v-Motor-Trade-Association.php

Hanly, An Introduction to Irish Criminal Law 2nd ed. (Dublin, 2006)

Hedley, Steve. 2012. Contract / Mistake. [ONLINE] Available at: http://www.stevehedley.com. [Accessed 17 July 15].

Hedley, Steve. 2012. Contract / Pressure [ONLINE] Available at: http://www.stevehedley.com. [Accessed 17 July 15].

Herring, Criminal Law: Text, Cases and Materials 4th ed (Oxford University Press, 2010).

Holmes O'Malley Sexton, Bishopsgate, Henry Street, Limerick, Ireland,. 2013.

High Court Ruling on Undue Influence (15.11.2013). [ONLINE] Available at: http://www.homs.ie/whatsnew-publication-367-High_Court_Ruling_on_Undue_Influence_(15.11.2013). [Accessed 11 November 14].

Hong Kong Land Law Blog. 2013. Barclays Bank plc v O'Brien: the risk of failing to take steps to ensure informed consent. [ONLINE] Available at: https://hklandlaw.wordpress.com/2013/10/01/barclays-bank-plc-v-obrien-the-risk-of-failing-to-take-steps-to-ensure-informed-consent/. [Accessed 11 November 14].

Ireland, P. (2012, july). Vicarious Liability. Retrieved January 2, 2015, from Peninsula Ireland: https://thepeninsulairelandblog.wordpress.com/2012/07/25/vicarious-liability-implications-for-employers/

IRISH LAW: A STUDENT'S GUIDE (2012) IRISH LEGAL SYSTEM [accessed 2 June 2011]. https://lawinireland.wordpress.com/irish-legal-system/

IRISH LAW: A STUDENT'S GUIDE (2012) CONTRACT LAW [accessed 2 June 2011]. https://lawinireland.wordpress.com/the-law-of-contract/

Keenan, A. (2008) Essentials of Irish Business Law, Fifth Edition, Dublin, Gill and Macmillan.

Lawteacher.Net. 2013. Exclusion Clauses Cases. [ONLINE] Available at: http://www.lawteacher.net/cases/contract-law/exclusion-clauses-cases.php. [Accessed 22 September 15].

Irish Statute Book. (2009). Criminal Justice (Public Order) Act, 1994. Retrieved 2012, from Irish Statute Book, : http://www.irishstatutebook.ie/eli/1994/act/2/section/8/enacted/en/html

Irish Statute Book. (2009). Criminal Justice (Public Order) Act, 1994. Retrieved 2011, from Irish Statute Book: http://www.irishstatutebook.ie/eli/1994/act/2/section/9/enacted/en/html

Irish Statute Book. (2010). Criminal Justice Act 2006. Retrieved 2012, from Irish Statute Book: http://www.irishstatutebook.ie/eli/2006/act/26/section/184/enacted/en/html

Irish Statute Book. (2014). Criminal Justice (Public Order) Act 2011. Retrieved 2014, from Irish Statute Book: http://www.irishstatutebook.ie/eli/2011/act/5/section/2/enacted/en/html

Irish Statute Book S14. (n.d.). Criminal Justice (Public Order) Act, 1994. Retrieved from Irish Statute Book: http://www.irishstatutebook.ie/eli/1994/act/2/section/14/enacted/en/html

Irish Statute Book S15. (2012). Section 15 of the Criminal Justice (Public Order) Act 1994 . Retrieved 2013, from Irish Statute Book: http://www.irishstatutebook.ie/eli/1994/act/2/section/15/enacted/en/html

Irish Statute Book S16. (2010). Criminal Justice (Public Order) Act, 1994. Retrieved 2012, from Irish Statute Book: http://www.irishstatutebook.ie/eli/1994/act/2/section/16/enacted/en/html

Irish Statute book, S. (2009). Criminal Justice Act (Public order) Act 1994. Retrieved 2011, from Irish Statute Book: http://www.irishstatutebook.ie/eli/1994/act/2/section/18/enacted/en/html

Mason Hayes and Curran. 2012. Taking security: the problem of "vulnerable" guarantors [ONLINE] Available at: http://www.mhc.ie/latest/e-zines/litigation-risk-update august-2012/P1. [Accessed 01 February 16].

McIntyre, McMullan and O Toghda, Criminal Law (Dublin, 2012)

McAuley and McCutcheon, Criminal liability: A Grammar (Dublin, 2000).

Ormerod, Smith and Hogan Criminal Law, 13th ed. (Oxford University Press, 2011).

O'Malley, Sexual Offences 2nd ed. (Dublin, 2013).

Possible offences. (n.d.). Retrieved from http://www.freebeagles.org/ALP/offences.htm

Section 185 of the Criminal Justice Act, 2. (2012). Section 19 of the Criminal Justice (Public Order) Act 1994. Retrieved 2012, from Irish Statute Book: http://www.irishstatutebook.ie/eli/1994/act/2/section/19/enacted/en/html

Tompkin (2014) [ONLINE] Last accessed 2 July 2012 www.jsijournal.ie/.../4%5B2%5D_Tomkin

Wikia Case Briefs. 2010. Case Law Thornton v Shoe Lane Parking Ltd.. [ONLINE] Available at: http://casebrief.wikia.com/wiki/Thornton_v_Shoe_Lane_Parking_Ltd.. [Accessed 02 September 14].

Wikipedia. 2012. Barton v Armstrong. [ONLINE] Available at: https://en.wikipedia.org/wiki/Barton_v_Armstrong. [Accessed 08 October 15].

Wikipedia. 2011. Edgington v Fitzmaurice - Misrepresentation. [ONLINE] Available at: https://en.wikipedia.org/wiki/Edgington_v_Fitzmaurice. [Accessed 01 February 16].

Woods, Kieron (2011) The Irish Legal System [ONLINE] Last accessed 2 July 2012 http://irishbarrister.com/legalterms.html

2012. [online] assessed 1 April 2013 www.gcc.ie/files/20090519051644_Chapter%2002_Criminal.pdf

2012. [online] assessed 1 April 2013 http://en.wikipedia.org/wiki/Conspiracy_(crime)

2012. [online] assessed 1 April 2013 http://en.wikipedia.org/wiki/Attempt

2012. [online] assessed 1 April 2013 http://www.higginsclaims.com/PIAB/Irish_Courts_System/irish_courts_system.html

2012. [online] assessed 1 April 2013 http://www.courts.ie

2012. [online] assessed 1 April 2013 http://www.probation.ie/pws/websitepublishingdec09.nsf/Content/Irish+Criminal+Justice+System2

2012. [online] assessed 1 April 2013 http://www.dppireland.ie/filestore/documents/Chapter_2_The_Prosecution_System_in_Ireland.htm

2012. [online] assessed 1 April 2013 http://www.citizensinformation.ie/en/justice/courts_system/

2012. [online] assessed 1 April 2013 http://businessandlegal.ie/criminal-law-in-ireland-the-prosecution-of-crime

2012. [online] assessed 1 April 2013 http://www.citizensinformation.ie/en/justice/arrests/arrests.html

2012. [online] assessed 1 April 2013 http://www.citizensinformation.ie/en/justice/criminal_law/criminal_offences/drug_offences.html

2012. [online] assessed 1 April 2013 http://bestirishfacts.com/capitalpunishment.html

2012. [online] assessed 1 April 2013 Aug. 20, 2007 - BBC (British Broadcasting Corporation)

2012. [online] assessed 1 April 2013 http://freepages.genealogy.rootsweb.ancestry.com/~irishancestors/Law/TFO/Sample.html

2012. [online] assessed 1 April 2013 http://www.citizensinformation.ie/en/health/mental_health/criminal_insanity_and_mental_health.html

2012. [online] assessed 1 April 2013 www.lawreform.ie/_.../Duress%20and%20Necessity%20CP.pdf

2012. [online] assessed 1 April 2013 http://insanityplea.umwblogs.org/standards/the-mnaghten-rule/

An Introduction to Criminal Law in Ireland

About the Author:

Teresa obtained her BA (Hons)LLB in 2005 she worked in legal investigations such as Miscarriage of Justice on behalf of clients who were either incarcerated or being charged with crimes they claimed they did not commit. She obtained a Masters in Criminology and Criminal Psychology in 2013 and has attended many seminars on criminal behaviour as well as numerous TV appearances.

An Irish writer of children's fiction and adults plain English legal and forensic psychology academic books. Teresa has been a private investigator, writer, photographer and lecturer, she backpacked around Europe with her daughter, sails a lovely boat called Baby Girl and survived a scuba diving accident.

A Law lecturer and Forensic Psychology lecturer by profession, in a previous life Teresa moonlight as a Private "I", and a photojournalist, having written for many local and national papers and magazines including the Mullingar Advertiser, Irish News Review, crime.ie and Emerald Road Racing.

Teresa is a registered member of the Teaching Council of Ireland. She has over 9 years' experience in teaching law and recognised the need for a beginners guide to law as she witnessed how the terminology and principles were hard work for some new students.

Despite or in spite of that fact that Teresa is a proud Aspie, diagnosed in 2007 with Asperger Syndrome, she loves to read and has favourites in the classics such as Ulysses by James Joyce, Oliver Twist and David Copperfield by Charles Dickens, Roddy Doyle is a long term favourite of Teresa's. If you want to connect to Teresa you can go to http://www.facebook.com/cypathia; twitter @cypathia, or if you would like to know when Teresa's next book will come out, please visit her website at http://www.teresaclyne.com, where you can sign up to receive an email when she has her next release.